Glorious Splendor

THE
18th-Century Wallpapers
IN THE
Jeremiah Lee Mansion
IN MARBLEHEAD, MASSACHUSETTS

Judy Anderson

The Donning Company Publishers
184 Business Park Drive, Suite 206
Virginia Beach, VA 23462

    Steve Mull, General Manager
    Barbara Buchanan, Office Manager
    Pamela Koch, Senior Editor
    Amanda Dawn Guilmain, Graphic Designer
    Priscilla Odango, Imaging Artist
    Susan Adams, Project Coordinator
    Tonya Washam, Marketing Specialist
    Pamela Engelhard, Marketing Advisor

    Mary Miller, Project Director

Library of Congress Cataloging-in-Publication Data

Anderson, Judy, 1957–
  Glorious splendor : the 18th-century wallpapers in the Jeremiah Lee Mansion in Marblehead, Massachusetts / by Judy Anderson.
    p. cm.
  Includes bibliographical references.
  ISBN 978-1-57864-668-5 (soft cover : alk. paper)
  1. Wallpaper–England–History–18th century. 2. Interior walls–Decoration–Massachusetts–Marblehead.
3. Jeremiah Lee Mansion (Marblehead, Mass.) I. Title. II. Title: Eighteenth-century wallpapers in the Jeremiah Lee Mansion in Marblehead, Massachusetts.
  NK3443.A53 2011
  676'.2848097445–dc22
             2010051589

Printed in the United States of America at Walsworth Publishing Company

Images of the Lee Mansion interiors and objects on display are courtesy of the Marblehead Museum & Historical Society (MMHS), Marblehead, MA, which has owned the house since 1909.

Photographs of the Lee Mansion and its interiors and wallpapers were taken by Judy Anderson, unless otherwise indicated. Cover photograph by Lucinda Lambton, London.

Glorious Splendor

The 18th-Century Wallpapers in the Jeremiah Lee Mansion in Marblehead, Massachusetts

by Judy Anderson

MMHS

CONTENTS

PREFACE

The magnificent original 1760s hand-painted scenic wallpapers in the Jeremiah Lee Mansion in Marblehead, Massachusetts—a thriving seaport that was one of the ten largest towns in America on the eve of independence—are a remarkable survival. One of only two sets in the world now in existence, they are the only ones still in their original context and placement, in one of America's most outstanding late colonial homes.

These significant and nearly unique historic wallpapers are among the most impressive interior embellishments from late colonial America.

In the Lee family's grand residence, they were complemented by colorful printed wall coverings that are now virtually unknown. The variety of their patterns represents in large measure the range of interior decorative finishes that were available to colonial American consumers at that time. Together with the scenic mural papers, those rare vestiges of pattern and color in early American homes reveal what would have been a dramatic interior design effect. Today, they comprise one of the largest collections of mid-eighteenth-century English wallpapers in America.

Scholars of history, architecture, and interiors visit the mansion from both around and outside the country, for it is rare to find, on either side of the Atlantic, such an impressive and extensive decorative scheme still in the place for which it was intended.

SCENIC PANELS framed by asymmetrical scrollwork enhance the mansion's grandest rooms (left). They were accented by large design emblems like this example (right), prominently placed on the landing of the main staircase, with an eagle and shield emblazoned with a figure enthroned, set above a compass and square— perhaps symbolic allusions to Colonel Lee and his grand architectural achievement with his glorious mansion. *MMHS*

For the first time in a publication dedicated just to them, this book illuminates the exceptional Lee Mansion wallpapers and provides information about them. A chapter also discusses the origins and manufacture of the papers, as well as other related papers: in a period room in the Metropolitan Museum of Art's American Wing, in an eighteenth-century doll house in London, a home in Albany that once had them, and a plan for scenic papers drawn by Patriot Benjamin Franklin's natural son William, a Loyalist and the last royal governor of New Jersey, who requested but never got them.

The Lee Mansion is an American treasure that would have inspired awe in its time, and still does today. This book will give readers insights into these remarkable papers—though it cannot compare with experiencing the splendor of the Lee Mansion's magnificent interiors first-hand.

Also compelling is the story of its original and only individual resident owner, Colonel Jeremiah Lee, whose business acumen and accomplishments brought the mansion into being—just moments, so to speak, before he sacrificed all of it for the cause of American independence.

With the exquisite wallpapers creating a visual setting unlike any other in America, and Colonel Lee's intriguing and unsung Patriot story, visiting the Lee Mansion in the pleasant days of summer or early autumn is an experience nearly unmatched, and not to be missed. This informative book would be a fitting complement to a visit to seaside Marblehead and the exceptional Jeremiah Lee Mansion.

INTRODUCTION

THE LEE MANSION AND ITS WALLPAPERS

"The Lee Mansion is one of the grandest Georgian houses in America, and the wallpapers related to it are among the most important to survive from the 18th century. Together with the pieces from several different patterns of block-printed wallpaper that Lee apparently ordered from England at the same time for other rooms of the house, the Lee Mansion wallpapers form an unparalleled document of 18th-century taste preserved in one American house."

Richard C. Nylander
Curator Emeritus, Historic New England

❮ THE LEE MANSION'S RESPLENDENT ORIGINAL HAND-PAINTED SCENIC WALLPAPERS are among the most spectacular interior embellishments surviving from America's late colonial era, just prior to independence. Together with virtuoso woodwork carving, they presented a vision of opulence and artistry that was matched by few homes at that time. *MMHS*

The magnificent original 1760s hand-painted English scenic wallpapers in the Jeremiah Lee Mansion in Marblehead, Massachusetts, are among the most spectacular interior embellishments to survive from late colonial America, just prior to the nation's independence.

Exceptionally rare both then and now, the fragile mural papers have distinction as one of only two sets in the world like them, and the only such mural papers still in their original location. Still resplendent two and a half centuries later, the scenic mural papers were at the apex of fashion for colonial America.

THE JEREMIAH LEE MANSION IN MARBLEHEAD, MASSACHUSETTS, was one of the largest and most highly finished houses of its day, and is today considered to be one of the finest homes from just before American independence.

The grand residence for which they were designed and in which they so uniquely survive was built for Colonel Jeremiah Lee, a ship-owner and merchant in the trans-Atlantic fish trade in the flourishing seaport of Marblehead just prior to the American Revolution. It was constructed in 1766–68 as a new full-time residence for his family, twenty years into his marriage and twenty-five years after he arrived in Marblehead at age twenty-one to begin his mercantile career. The Lees' "mansion house," as fine homes were often called at that time, was one of the largest, most opulent, and highly finished houses of its generation.

Surviving nearly intact, it is today considered to be one of the most superlative houses from its era.

Colonel Lee was a prominent leader in his community and one of the most affluent men in Britain's North American colonies, with one of the largest fleets of fishing and trading vessels in late colonial America. By the time the mansion was complete, according to a 1771 tax listing, Lee was one of the wealthiest men in Massachusetts, until he sacrificed everything—his fortune, his home, and his life—to the cause of independence, just as the Revolution began.

But in the few short years before his significant but largely unknown support of the Revolution, before and early in the rebellion, the Lee family's majestic new residence was furnished and ornamented with some of the best craftsmanship available to late-colonial America's thriving gentry class: fine furnishings, rich textiles and upholstery, radiant looking glasses, fine silver and ceramics, and walls profusely ornamented with bold colors, lively patterns, and dramatic imagery—with the scenic murals as the zenith of interior splendor on western Atlantic shores.

Combined with the monumental scale of the house, the mural papers created "a statement of remarkable impact, and still articulate the high-style sensibilities of early Americans in an extraordinarily striking way," according to Margaret Pritchard, wallpaper curator and historic house consultant at the Colonial Williamsburg Foundation in Virginia. "In no other place can so many colonial wallpapers and patterns be seen in the context for which they were designed."

Important in their own right as rare aesthetic artifacts, the wallpapers are also extremely valuable as exceptional historical documents of eighteenth-century craftsmanship and taste, as well as patterns of consumption and interior design in early America.

> *"Beyond their intrinsic artistic merit, these wallpapers provide insights about colonial Americans at a time when they were actively asserting their spirit of independence. "*
>
> **Margaret Pritchard**
> **Curator of Maps, Prints, and Wallpapers,**
> **Colonial Williamsburg Foundation**

CLEARLY DESIGNED FOR GRAND ENTERTAINMENTS, the mansion's spacious rooms were public spaces for hosting receptions, dining parties, assemblies, or balls—a virtual stage upon which gentility could be paraded or played, as customary in the best houses at that time. *MMHS*

IMMENSE PORTRAITS of Jeremiah Lee and his wife Martha by John Singleton Copley clearly confirmed their stature in the community and were doubtless commissioned to celebrate the completion of their new residence. The present images are late 1800s copies donated by Lee descendants, situated in what are thought to be their original locations. *MMHS*

WITH THEIR GRAND SCALE, the portraits and wallpaper scenes emulated aristocratic houses in England, where large likenesses and paintings covered the walls. The rococo silhouette of the gilt wood frames mirrored the scrollwork around the wallpaper images. *Photo by Marcia J. Hunkins. MMHS*

Both portraits now in the Mansion are nineteenth-century copies commissioned for Lee descendant Elizabeth Amory Ernst, and donated by her granddaughter Elizabeth Morton Grinnell and husband George Grinnell. MMHS Collection

The original portraits by John Singleton Copley are in the Wadsworth Atheneum, Hartford, Connecticut.

The papers were enhanced by elaborate interior woodwork that includes intricate carving in an exuberant rococo style in the large entry hall and dining parlors, and an extensive expanse of mahogany wall paneling throughout the spacious stair-hall, upstairs and down—all masterfully executed and conceived.

The ornament of the papers and carved woodwork combined to create what Morrison Heckscher, chairman of the American Wing at the Metropolitan Museum of Art in New York City, has called "the ultimate expression of architectural rococo in Massachusetts."[1]

Crowning the staircase, at the pinnacle of the view as one entered, a full-length portrait of Colonel Lee by the leading artist of the day, John Singleton Copley, proclaimed his status in the community, as portraits often did. Just opposite, and complementing his commanding presence, an equally regal portrait of his wife visually welcomed guests into the brilliant upper realm of their home with gentle grace.[2] In gilt wood frames nearly ten feet tall,[3] the portraits were two of only four full-length portraits of standing adults in the entire production of that prolific artist until he left America for England a few years later.[4] They embodied the gentility the Lees sought to convey through their painted likenesses as well as through the elegance of their home and its accoutrements.

In addition to the scenic murals, other papers graced the walls of other rooms in the Lee Mansion as well—apparently seven different patterns of English block-printed papers. Large pieces of six of those still exist, preserved in the archives of the Marblehead Museum & Historical Society, which has owned and cared for the Lee Mansion since 1909. Together with four patterns of borders, which are particularly scarce, they comprise one of the largest collections of colonial-period wallpapers in America. Fragments of a seventh, in the collection of the Cooper-Hewitt, National Design Museum, hint at its original beauty.

A HIGH-STYLE PRINTED WALLPAPER WITH CHINESE MOTIFS, still uniquely in place, was one of seven different patterns of block-printed English wallpapers that were apparently in the Lee Mansion, in addition to the scenic mural papers. Those printed patterns comprise one of the finest collections of mid-1700s wallpapers in America, particularly as related to one building. *MMHS Collection, in situ*

The printed papers are very important, especially as apparently all from one house. But despite that, those printed or "stampt" wallpapers, as they were often advertised in the 1760s, are virtually unknown—partially due to the prominence of the scenic mural papers. And other than two articles in respected national antiques magazines, in 1979 and 2009,[5] no publication has specifically discussed the scenic mural papers, or brought to light the rare and beautiful block-printed papers. The purpose of this book is to illuminate all of the extraordinary wallpaper related to this house, and to celebrate those jewels in the Lee Mansion's abundance of outstanding artistry and craftsmanship.

The Lee Mansion survives so remarkably intact because after the Lee family's residency and ownership—which effectively ended in 1775 and 1785 respectively, with the death of Lee and then his eldest son and heir, who lived in the family's former home nearby—the house had only two nominal mortgage holders until 1804, followed by only two principal owners, each for an entire century and one of them beyond, through the 1800s and 1900s. Both were conscientious, prudent, and respectful of the mansion's integrity and history. From 1804 to 1904, the house was owned by and operated as a bank and office building. And since 1909, it has been owned, maintained, and preserved by the Marblehead Historical Society, now called the Marblehead Museum & Historical Society.

THE LEE MANSION SURVIVED VIRTUALLY INTACT over two and a half centuries because for one hundred years through the 1800s it was owned by a bank that made few changes to the building while maintaining it conscientiously until the house was purchased in 1909 by the Marblehead Historical Society. *Photo c. 1850–70, Collection of Dr. Keith Taylor*

With continued careful stewardship, these unique and remarkable vestiges of a vanished time can last for centuries to come, to articulate with visual eloquence the artistry of their age and the story of those who brought them into being.

MARBLEHEAD'S COLONIAL PROSPERITY was built on North Atlantic fishing and the production and trade in dried salt fish, primarily cod. On sturdy two-masted fishing schooners, rugged crews of ten to twenty men each braved the storms, waves, and frigid waters of the North Atlantic for a month or two per voyage to harvest their prodigious catch of large, heavy fish by hand-lining directly over the sides of the pitching boats. Salted in the hold, the fish were brought back to be cleaned and then dried for weeks on the rocky headlands surrounding Marblehead's deep-water harbor. Trading vessels brought the dried fish down the coast, to the West Indies in the Caribbean, or across the Atlantic Ocean to ports in Spain, Portugal, and the nearby islands. From that commercial industry, the seaport of Marblehead grew to about the tenth largest town in America for a decade or two just before the Revolution.

VIEW OF THE TOWN OF MARBLEHEAD, MASSACHUSETTS.

ENGRAVING: Fish flanks dry on racks or "flakes" set out on the granite headlands along the rocky shore of Marblehead's harbor. *Gleason's Pictorial Drawing-Room Companion*, June 17, 1854, page 276, artist unknown. *Author's collection*

FIREBOARD: This wooden fireboard painted in oil, for placement in front of a fireplace in the warm months of summer, depicts two schooners anchored at the base of Marblehead Harbor, with part of the Great Neck in the background, c. 1801, artist unknown. *MMHS Collection*

PAINTING: Crewmen hauled large fish caught on a series of hooks on long lines while leaning over the sides of the schooner, as customary at that time, as the vessel rolls in heavy North Atlantic waves. *A Smart Blow*, 1856, Mary Blood Mellen after Fitz Henry Lane. *Courtesy Cape Ann Museum, Gloucester, MA*

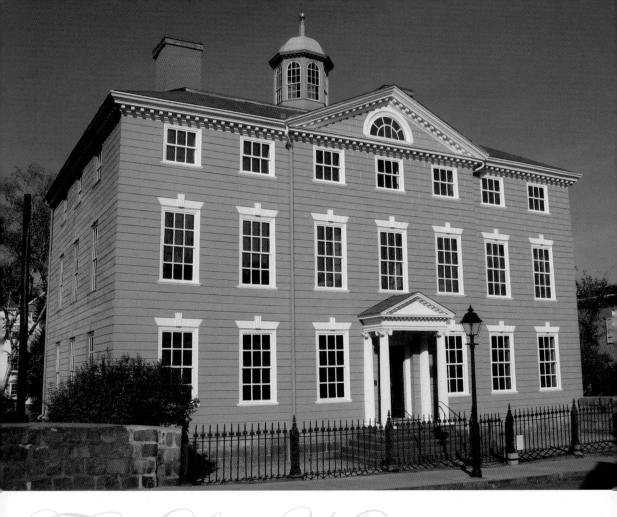

THE LEE MANSION

One of the largest and most highly finished houses from late colonial America, the Jeremiah Lee Mansion in Marblehead, Massachusetts, on the seacoast north of Boston, was built in 1766–68 for Colonel Jeremiah Lee, one of the wealthiest men in Britain's North American colonies at that time.[6] In the 1760s, both Lee and his adopted town were at the pinnacle of their commercial prosperity, and Marblehead was among the ten largest towns in America. Its population of nearly five thousand[7] was densely settled along one mile by about a half-mile at the northeast tip of a rocky peninsula that was bounded to the east by a deep-water harbor. Its economy was based on the arduous harvesting of, and overseas Atlantic trade in, dried salt fish—primarily, but not exclusively, North Atlantic cod (see page 84).

Emulating an aristocratic English stone house, the Lee Mansion was built of New England wood that was fashioned on all four facades of the immense structure to simulate cut stone ashlar blocks. Crowned by its large octagonal cupola, the mansion includes three full floors with a full attic above; granite foundation blocks enclose a brick-floored cellar with seven-foot ceilings. A balustrade once added elegance to the gable-on-hip roof, but was removed in the 1800s.

Colonel Jeremiah Lee

was one of the most affluent men in Britain's North American colonies. A merchant and ship-owner in New England's Atlantic trade in dried salt fish, primarily cod, Lee was the owner of one of the largest fleets of vessels in colonial America. A prominent citizen and civic leader before the Revolution, he also held respected positions in the regional provincial Massachusetts government. He was appointed as a colonel in the Marblehead militia in 1751, at age thirty. That same year he and his wife Martha, married for six years, moved into their first fine house, located around the corner from where their grand mansion would later be built. Their six children (of nine born) would be raised in that house.[8] And it was there that Lee built the far-reaching Atlantic shipping empire that would make him the wealthiest merchant in Massachusetts by the time or soon after their new mansion was complete. Just a few short years later, however, Colonel Lee would risk and sacrifice the family's lavish new mansion as well as his life for America's independence.

COLONEL JEREMIAH LEE (1721–1775), age 47, c. 1768/9. *Portrait by John Singleton Copley (1738–1815) The Ella Gallup Sumner and Mary Catlin Sumner Collection Fund 1945.58, Courtesy Wadsworth Atheneum Museum of Art, Hartford, Connecticut/Art Resource, NY*

FOR SIXTEEN YEARS BEFORE their grand new residence was built, the Lee family lived in this fine "mansion house"[9] with their six children, of nine born. And it was here that Lee, named a colonel when he moved into this house in 1751, built his Atlantic shipping empire.

The recessed corner was part of the house's original construction in 1731; it originally accommodated the door to a shop for retail goods located in that room well into the 1800s, on what would have been a busy street corner in the 1700s, near the major wharves.

When construction began on the Lee Mansion in 1766, less than a decade before the outbreak of the American Revolution, Marblehead was a flourishing commercial seaport, the second-largest town in Massachusetts and among the ten largest towns in Britain's North American colonies. (Lee Mansion in center) *Photo by Dennis Curtin*

Colonel Lee, his wife Martha, and his family of five or six surviving children were certainly well established in their grand new residence by 1768, twenty-three years after their marriage. Their eldest son had already left home to attend Harvard in Cambridge, and his marriage in 1771 was celebrated with a gala event at the mansion attended by many. Four years later, the Lees' oldest daughter would wed one of the wealthiest young men in Newburyport.

Inside

The Lee Mansion was one of the most highly finished and opulently appointed American dwellings of its time. Surviving virtually intact over two and a half centuries, it retains much of its outstanding original craftsmanship and high-style ornament, including intricate interior woodwork carving in the flamboyant rococo style, transfer-printed English ceramic fireplace tiles, and rare mahogany wall paneling in the grand stair-hall, upstairs and down,[10] in concert with the splendid painted wall coverings.

In the best parlor, the blaze of carving around the marble-framed fireplace was a tour-de-force of rococo embellishment, akin to the wallpapers originally in the entry-hall adjacent, and is considered to be some of the best carving from its time in America.[11]

The elaborate rococo carving around the chimney-breast in the best parlor and the *trompe l'oeil* scrollwork of the wallpapers in the entry-hall adjacent were likely complemented by large mirrors or "looking glasses" on the walls between the four large windows, which would have brought added brilliance to the parlor, originally with an ochre yellow or "stone" color paint treatment. Perhaps they were the two pairs of high-valued "carved gilt looking glasses" listed on Colonel Lee's probate inventory.

THE METICULOUSLY CARVED cornice molding at the ceiling, with seven rows of minute dentils, includes three-inch modillion blocks that were diminutive versions of the stair-brackets. *MMHS*

THE LARGE BEST PARLOR, fully paneled in pine that was originally a yellow ocher color (as in photo at right), would have been the scene of elegant dinner parties or dancing at an "assembly" or ball.[12] The current simulated oak-grained decorative paint treatment throughout the room from 1852 is singular in its own right, and a noteworthy part of the mansion's history. The elaborate chimney-breast is a blaze of intricate rococo carving based directly on two English pattern book designs.
MMHS, Photo by Robert D. Mussey Jr.

THE WOODWORK IN THE FRONT PARLOR was originally painted the same buff yellow ocher color as the stair landing woodwork shown in this detail above.
MMHS, Photo by Rick Ashley

❯ THE FASHIONABLE GREY-AND-WHITE color scheme of the scenic papers, called *grisaille*, was inspired by the prints and engravings that were popular among art collectors and connoisseurs in both England and America at that time. *MMHS*

TRIOS OF TWIST-TURNED BALUSTERS swirl upward in three different patterns above the intricately carved stair-brackets, which are among the most elaborate from colonial America. *MMHS, Photo by Alex McLean*

THIS EIGHTEENTH-CENTURY LOOKING GLASS has a history of ownership in the family of the Lees' eldest daughter Mary, so it is tempting to speculate that it could perhaps have been inherited from her father.[13] *Courtesy Historical Society of Old Newbury, Massachusetts*

THE EXQUISITE ACANTHUS-LEAF CARVING of the ornamental brackets at the end of each stair riser on the main staircase echoes the scrollwork framing the wallpapers, and is based on two designs in the same British pattern book that was the design source for the chimney-breast and its elaborate carving.[14] *Both photos MMHS, top photo by Geoffrey Gross for Great Houses of New England, Rizzoli, NY*

THE SCENIC MURAL PAPERS

The Lee Mansion is best known for its splendid wallpapers with grand scenes painted in shades of grey highlighted with white. Like other consumer luxuries such as shimmering silk textiles or silver household wares—more opulent even than fine English-made goods like harrateen upholstery cloth, Chinese-inspired ceramics, or colorful block-printed wallpapers—painted scenic papers like these conferred particular prestige upon their owners.

The chiaroscuro scenes, with modeling in light and dark tones to give them three-dimensional effects of depth and shadow, were painted *en grisaille* (a French term pronounced *griss-eye*, meaning "in varying tones of grey"), and framed by elaborate painted *rocaille* scrollwork (again French, meaning "rock-like, grotto-esque, or shell-like"), with scalloped flourishes that simulated decoratively carved plasterwork. The tops and bottoms of the frames were accented by sculptural *trompe l'oeil* shells ("fooling the eye" or trying to appear real, usually in a two-dimensional format). Above the doorways into the rooms, smaller panels feature baskets of fruit or flowers, and from above the door to the best parlor, just as one enters the mansion, a face peers out in a mannerist mode (see page 90, Photo Credits).[15]

An impressive artistic creation and an equally remarkable survival, the mural papers remain in place throughout the upper central stair-hall and into the two large second-floor front rooms, and once extended throughout the lower entry hall as well.

The papers were hand-painted in London by specially trained artisans called "paper stainers"—though the term "stainers" or "stayners" and "stained" seems to have been used for either painted or printed wallpaper.

LARGE SCENIC PANELS are framed by *trompe l'oeil* scrollwork in a rococo mode, whose chiaroscuro shadows of light and dark create a three-dimensional effect.

Painted freehand, these murals are particularly unusual because most wallpapers were printed rather than painted, with the decorative patterns printed or "stamped" in successive layers by wooden blocks onto a uniform background color that was pre-painted onto rolls of hand-made paper, in a repeating design that was often fairly large (though not always), and typically based on or inspired by textile patterns.

The grand scale of the Lee mural papers, their classical imagery, and the fact that they were hand-painted rather than printed, would have distinguished them as exceptional in their day. Even luxury wallpapers occasionally promoted in newspaper advertisements or described on merchants' orders as *landskips* were most likely large-format printed papers, with complex imagery in many colors from many blocks for each large repeating scene.[16] Generally made for spaces smaller than the Lees' lofty walls, those landscapes would not have been surrounded by a framework other than the borders along the edges. And though "Sundry sorts of Painted Paper for Rooms" was advertised to be sold in Boston as early as 1738,[17] it is likely that those papers were actually printed. In 1752, a published notice announced "Landscapes printed in Colours" by John Baptist Jackson, whom it described as a "Reviver of the Art of printing in Chiaro Oscuro." A master woodcutter and printer in London, Jackson wrote a treatise entitled *An Essay on the Invention of Engraving and Printing in Chiaro Oscuro*, which discussed the printing of scenic imagery, and produced "paper hangings printed in "Oyl."[18]

For the Lees' and the other known set of painted mural papers, however, the scenes were painted freehand,[19] in water-based tempera, or distemper, into which powdered whitening and charcoal, lampblack, or other darkening pigments were ground. And the entire scheme was custom designed for their homes.[20]

THE PANELS WERE ACCENTED by artistic devices or "trophy" designs with architectural, military, or pastoral agrarian themes, seen on this page and opposite. *Both MMHS*

YARDS OF PRINTED EGG-AND-DART BORDERS mirror the woodwork moldings around windows and doorways. *MMHS*

The overall effect of the framed scenic panels accented by the ornamental frames and "trophies"— "tripoly's" on a 1761 invoice[21]—suggested the appearance of an eighteenth-century "print room," popular in the 1700s across the Atlantic and seen sometimes in America as well, in which engravings were displayed against a solid color on the walls of a room, surrounded by ornamental paper frames and cartouches. Rolled wallpapers printed with small images in frames with cartouches and other framing devices were also popular.[22] In the case of these mural papers, however, the images were much larger than typical in most print rooms or on printed wallpapers that simulated them.

The painted images on the papers depict classical scenes that were based on European paintings reproduced by English, French, Dutch, German, or Italian engravers.[23] As a researcher at the Marblehead Historical Society, Narcissa Chamberlain, wrote in 1971, "Paintings of the romantic school by European artists were much in vogue in the 18th century, and many English engravers made black and white engravings after these subjects."[24] In 1773, a variety of block-printed wallpapers as well as hand-painted scenic murals on paper *"represented in black and white in Imitation of Copper Plate on a Buff coloured ground from the Prints of those Falls sold by Jeffereys . . . painted or stained"*[25] were requested for the residence provided for the governor of New Jersey (see pages 30–31).

THE SCENIC PANELS framed by the faux scrollwork and accented by ornamental "trophies" suggested the appearance of an eighteenth-century print room, but in grander scale. Fully printed wallpapers with architectural themes or smaller framed scenes that evoked a print-room appearance were also available, but were not chosen for this house. *MMHS*

In the Lee Mansion, the most formal scenes depicted Greek and Roman buildings, generally in a state of noble ruin. In the mid-1700s, the aristocracy and the merchant and professional classes in all of Europe, including England and her global colonies, were enamored of classical architecture, imagery, and ideas. This wall imagery brought the Lee family into the mainstream of contemporary taste in England and Europe, where the fascination for ruins was at its peak.[26]

Herculaneum and Pompeii in particular had been rediscovered in 1738 and 1748, and those sites had an especially strong influence on the neoclassical designs of the Adam Brothers and others in England after the 1750s. Those new visual interpretations of classical art and architecture (the new or "neo"-classical) were lighter and more attenuated expressions of the classical elements incorporated into earlier baroque or Georgian design for buildings, furniture, or interiors.

In the more public entertaining spaces, including the stair-hall and largest second-floor front chamber, scenes of Roman ruins were based on European engravings of paintings by Italian artist Gian Paolo Pannini (c. 1691–1764/5) and Pierre Antoine de Machy (1723-1807), a French painter of classical architecture scenes.[27] In the slightly less formal of the two front second-floor bedchambers, romanticized fishing and shipping scenes replicated French paintings by Joseph Vernet (1714–89).[28]

TOGETHER WITH THEIR *trompe l'oeil* frames and flanking design elements, the large scenic panels suggest the grand aristocratic paintings bordered by elaborate ornamental stucco or plasterwork seen in homes of the nobility in England and Europe, as in the parlor from Kirtlington Park in Oxfordshire, England, now in the Metropolitan Museum of Art. *Fletcher Fund, 1931 (32.53.1). Courtesy of the Metropolitan Museum of Art/Art Resource, NY*

GRAND SCENES OF ROMAN RUINS adorned the mansion's public entertaining rooms as architectural ruins and treasures coming to light in archaeological excavations in Greece and Italy during the 1600s and 1700s became models for artistic expression throughout Europe and England. *MMHS*

LESS FORMAL SCENES with more romantic themes adorned a room that was a more private, but still opulent, bedchamber—probably for the great fish merchant, Colonel Lee. Around this peaceful fishing scene, a Gothic-style trefoil border was apparently added later, in the 1800s. *MMHS*

OTHER 18TH-CENTURY ENGLISH PAINTED SCENIC MURAL PAPERS

Other than the Lee Mansion, only two other American houses from the colonial period are known to have had English painted mural papers. They were the grand mansions of two merchant landowners above the Hudson River on the outskirts of Albany, New York, a town somewhat smaller than Marblehead in the mid-1700s.[29] Only one of the two sets of papers survives, but the house it was in does not. The other house still exists, but without its original wallpapers.

Both of the Albany houses were large two-and-a-half-story residences built in the 1760s, as the Lee Mansion was, though it has three full floors. And like the Lee Mansion, both stretched seven window bays across instead of the more typical five, with spacious central entry halls, two window bays wide, that featured scenic wallpapers. In the surviving Albany mansion, similar in floor plan to the other, the mural papers may or may not have extended beyond the large central entry area and up into the large second-floor entertaining space, which the Albany merchant called a "saloon" in customary usage for the time.[30]

The Stephen Van Rensselaer Manor

One of the two New York mansions was built for young merchant Stephen Van Rensselaer in 1765–69, about the same time as Lee's, but was taken down in 1893.[31] The elaborately carved woodwork and painted mural papers of the opulent entry hall were removed, the papers rolled up and stored for thirty-five years, then donated to the Metropolitan Museum of Art in 1928. They were installed in the American Wing soon after, along with the woodwork and doors that had also been donated, to create the Van Rensselaer period room. One of the large scenic panels in that set is the same as an image that was formerly part of the suite of papers in the Lee Mansion's lower stair-hall, now lost. As in the Lee house, the largest scenes, both classical and romantic, were based on paintings by Pannini and Vernet, respectively. In the Van Rensselaer set, smaller panels depict landscape and seaport views, separated by

FROM ALBANY, NY

❮ THE ONLY OTHER SET of English painted *grisaille* mural papers surviving from the colonial period is a period room in the American Wing of the Metropolitan Museum of Art in New York City: the strikingly handsome central entry hall from the Stephen Van Rensselaer manor house just outside Albany, New York (1765–68), with its original carved woodwork and painted wallpapers. The current yellow color is a calcimine wash that was painted over the original light raw sienna (grey-brown toned) background, similar to the Lee Mansion's, sometime in the 1870s. *Great Hall of Van Rensselaer Manor House: woodwork and doors 1765–69, made in Albany, New York; wallpaper c. 1768, made in England. Gift of Mrs. William Bayard Van Rensselaer, in memory of her husband, 1928 (28.143—wallpaper & woodwork); Gift of Dr. Howard Van Rensselaer, 1928 (28.224—wallpaper); Gift of the Trustees of Sigma Phi Society of Williams College, 1931 (31.95.1-.2, .6—door & other woodwork). Courtesy of the Metropolitan Museum of Art / Art Resource, NY*

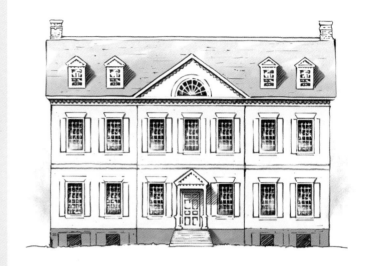

LIKE THE LEE MANSION, the Van Rensselaer manor house (built 1765–69) stretched seven windows across the front and was surmounted by an arched window within a triangular pediment at the roofline. The Van Rensselaer house sustained interior renovations, particularly in 1817 and 1843; exterior wings had been added, and the house was taken down in 1893 as the city grew. *Illustration by Jan Evans, after a drawing published by the Architects Emergency Committee, 1933*

The Van Rensselaer hall was repainted and reinstalled in 2011.

cartouches illustrating the four seasons, while the trophy panels flanking the doors at each end of the room represent the four elements: earth, fire, air, and water.[32] The *trompe l'oeil* scrollwork frames are lighter than those in the Lee Mansion, with lighter filigree, and some feature urns, birds, and cherubs; in the Lee house, shells centered at the tops and bottoms of the frames are the principal accent motif. A scene in the Van Rensselaer house depicting autumn is crowned with a basket of fruit that is very similar to a basket of flowers in a small panel over the door to one of the Lee Mansion rooms.[33]

The English painted *grisaille* papers and woodwork from the grand central entry hall of the manor house of Stephen Van Rensselaer were donated to the Metropolitan Museum of Art in 1928, along with a 1768 letter sent to the recently married young merchant from his powerful father-in-law, Philip Livingston, giving instructions for the careful unpacking of the rolls to ensure correct installation.[34]

The General Philip Schuyler Mansion

IN ALBANY, NY

Another house with classical scenic papers was the home of merchant landowner and future
Revolutionary War General Philip Schuyler and his family in Albany, New York. It is still standing
and is open to the public, though remodeled in the 1800s.[35] Although the mural papers from
that house were removed, probably in the 1870s, the invoice for Schuyler's purchase of them in
London reveals the manufactory for not only his papers, but also nearly certainly for those in the
Lee Mansion and from the manor house of Van Rensselaer, a Schuyler relation. All were built and
decorated in the same decade.[36] According to the invoice, Schuyler also purchased eight different
patterns in more than six colors of flock and "caffy" printed papers (actually "caffoy"—papers that
simulated damask fabrics of wool or silk, but sometimes also spelled "caffaw"), along with other
printed papers and accoutrements, including eighty dozen borders, "8 pieces Feston [festoon] Gothic
Stoco" [stucco, meaning papier-mâché imitating plasterwork] and twenty-four dozen "Stoco Borders"
as well as "10 Paintings ruins of Rome" and "1 Room—9 Ornaments of Pannells" in addition to "a
Neat Mache Ceiling to plan for a Room 25 ft by 20."[37]

THE SCHUYLER MANSION was built from 1761 to 1765, with some of the last elements (marble hearths and marble
fireplace facings) installed in 1767.[38] An exterior brick hexagonal enclosed entry portico was added later in the
Federal period,[39] and is still in place at the front of the house facing the Hudson River. *Drawing by unknown
artist, Courtesy Albany Public Library*

In General Schuyler's mansion in Albany, painted English scenic papers covered the upper wall spaces of this entry hall, and perhaps other formal areas of the house, and are thought to have survived into the 1870s. *Courtesy Schuyler Mansion State Historic Site, New York State Office of Parks, Recreation and Historic Preservation*

The mansion is open to the public. It is hoped that a facsimile of the painted wall coverings listed on Schuyler's 1761 invoice for wallpaper from the London manufactory of William Squire will be created at some point. Several of the documented flocked papers have already been reproduced.

The Proprietary House

Painted mural papers were envisioned for a fourth American house—the mansion provided for the governor in the port of Perth Amboy, in eastern New Jersey, just across from the southeast tip of Staten Island. The governor at that time, William Franklin (the last royal governor of New Jersey and estranged son of Benjamin Franklin due to their opposing views on the need for war with England in 1775), drew a plan for the various wallpapers he requested for the house—mostly printed wallpapers, but also including scenes of New York waterfalls "made on Purpose to suit the Pannels . . . " of the central entry "Hall."[40] Though printed papers were purchased for the other rooms in 1774, the request for the more expensive scenic murals was not fulfilled. Soon after, Governor Franklin was imprisoned by the rebel Patriot government, which took over the house.

Other premier American houses may have had scenic papers, whether urban residences in coastal American cities, or country houses or plantation homes on landed estates. On Staten Island, an advertisement for a house for sale in 1764 boasted a large parlor "hung with Landskip paper framed with papier machee."[41] Those landscape scenes may have been painted or printed, framed with either actual maché or printed faux papier-mâché borders.[42] But to date, no other actual painted scenic papers are known.[43]

THE PROPRIETARY HOUSE in Perth Amboy, New Jersey (1762–64), was provided for the use of the last royal governor appointed by the New Jersey governing body of Proprietors, William Franklin (son of the Patriot diplomat Benjamin Franklin). The house sustained a fire in the late 1700s; it was subsequently enlarged and remodeled as a hotel, but has been partially restored.[44] *Drawing above by unknown artist, Courtesy Proprietary House Association and State of New Jersey Department of Environmental Protection, Parks & Forestry*

THE GOVERNOR OF NEW JERSEY, William Franklin, drew, in ink, a floor plan in which he wrote the colors and types of patterns he preferred for each room in the house, specifying that the large central entry hall should feature murals with scenes of New York waterfalls on wallpaper *"made on Purpose to Suit the Pannels, Chimney &c . . . to have the Falls of Passaick & Cohoes represented . . . The same kind for the StairCase on which the Falls of Niagara to be painted or stained."*[45] Though the murals were not purchased, the surviving floor plan with handwritten notations sheds interesting light on eighteenth-century ideas about wallpaper color, pattern, and placement. *Memorandum of paper for the Proprietary House, 1774, Courtesy New Jersey State Archives*

The Proprietary House Association opens the house to the public and operates a weekly tea room.

THE DIMINUTIVE PARLOR of an engaging miniature Palladian-style town house, now in the Museum of London, features miniature *grisaille* scenes of ruins like the ones in the Lee Mansion. The Blackett family, for whom it was made after the birth of their son in 1759, was of the gentry class, but had gained a baronetcy based on their wealth accrued in the coal trade from their Northumberland mines.[46] *Courtesy Museum of London*

ABOVE THE PARLOR with the scenic *grisaille* papers, the delightful floral wallpaper in the upper chamber may resemble in both color and pattern the block-printed paper from the Lee Mansion that imitates an Indian "chints" textile pattern. *Courtesy Museum of London*

In England, painted *grisaille* papers like these were purchased not by members of the nobility, but by the gentry, professional and merchant classes, who were "anxious to show that they shared with the aristocracy a classical sensibility."[47] Their fine manor homes or town houses were smaller than aristocratic houses, just as fine gentry American homes were, and *grisaille* scenic murals were less costly than full-color panoramas, but more expensive than most repeating printed patterns. Gill Saunders, a curator of wallpapers at the Victoria & Albert Museum in London, wrote that in England, "most surviving examples [of scenic papers] are in the houses of rural notables [meaning leading citizens in smaller or mid-sized towns away from London, similar to Marblehead and Jeremiah Lee], since when used by an urban elite, the papers rarely survived the vagaries of fashion."[48]

Only two sets of painted scenic wallpapers are known to have persisted into the twentieth century in England; neither exists any longer. One of those two sets was in Harrington House, in Gloucestershire, built of local Cotswold stone as the home of a gentleman lawyer in the town of Bourton-on-the-Water. Like the Lee Mansion, its papers had scenes of classical ruins; they were likely removed in 1947 when the house was converted to a hotel. The other set was in a brick country house in Sussex called Hickstead Place, whose staircase featured images of hunting scenes rather than ruins, in shades of brown rather than grey. Its papers were removed by 1976.[49]

MANUFACTURER OF THE PAINTED SCENIC WALLPAPERS

The Lee Mansion wallpapers were very likely made in the London paper-staining manufactory of William Squire, a printer and retailer of wallpaper and decorative interior finishes. Squire's firm was also one of several factories or "mills" out of a few dozen in London that produced printed wallpapers in the mid-1700s, though only a few of those printed scenic panoramic or "landskip" papers. Advertisements for "paintings of landscapes" by other firms do exist, but Squire's is, to date, the only establishment specifically identified as having provided hand-painted scenic papers.[50]

THE LONDON "PAPER-STAINING" MANUFACTORY of William Squire, whose trade card is shown here, was one of several firms producing wallpaper in London, near St. Paul's churchyard, the center of the English wallpaper printing industry.[51] *Courtesy of the Trustees of the British Museum*

Scenic mural papers with framed panels were designed specifically for the walls of the grand home in which they would be installed. A drawing of the room plan, with doorways and wall elevations shown, would be sent to the manufactory along with the order for wallpapers, generally by way of a trading agent in London. At the workshop, the plan was marked with alphabetical letters noting the correct placement of the panels in the home, with titles of all the scenes listed on the plan keyed to the letters, then returned to the customer along with the finished papers. Corresponding letter notations were marked on each of the many rolls of papers that would have been sent out. For the Lee Mansion, handwritten pencil inscriptions on the back of the rolls also specified, in addition to the letters, the name of the scene and the room into which the rolls were to be installed. An example of such a plan, which came back to Albany patron Stephen Van Rensselaer with English mural papers ordered for him, was given to the Metropolitan Museum of Art by descendants, along with the wallpapers, after the house was taken down (see pages 26–27).[52]

PAPER MAKING

Paper made before the 1800s had a high linen or "rag" content since eighteenth-century paper was made of rags—generally worn linens or clothing. Soaked in vats of liquid to weaken the fibers, the fabrics were pounded to break down the fibers, forming a mash. The mix was then poured onto and through a flat screen held by a wooden framework; the fibers remaining on the screen formed a thin sheet of interwoven fibers that, when dried, created a sheet of crisp material or paper. In the American colonies, paper was a fairly expensive commodity, and was in particularly short supply during the Revolutionary War. Once wallpaper was made in America, after the Revolution, the paper made on the western shores of the Atlantic was heavier than paper made in England.[53]

MMHS

ON THE BACKS OF THE WALLPAPER rolls sent to Colonel Lee, room designations handwritten in ink (the words *Parlour Chamber*, as shown here, denoting the bedroom above the parlor) indicated the room for which that roll was destined, and an alphabetical letter (in this case, a C) identified the wall segment within the room onto which a particular series of rolls should be pasted. In some cases (as here, *"Temple of Venus"* on second line) the name of the scene created by the adjoining rolls was also written. This inscription was found on the back of papers in the Lee Mansion's smaller front second-floor chamber when they were removed during conservation in 1986–87. *MMHS Collection, in situ, Photo by T. K. McClintock, Northeast Document Conservation Center, North Andover, MA*

The paint medium was tempera or distemper, a type of water-soluble and fast-drying binding medium into which a colored pigment was ground. As customary, the paper support was a handmade "laid" paper.

By the 1700s, large sheets were glued together at both ends with overlapping horizontal seams to create a long stretch of paper that was rolled after being printed or painted (unlike earlier wallpapers, which were comprised of sets of single sheets of paper rather than rolls, that were pasted individually onto the walls—mainly before about 1712).[54] The finished wallpapers available for sale were often described in newspapers as "rolled" or "stampt" papers. For shipment abroad, the rolls were sold to trading agents in London who filled orders from England or America, Bermuda or Barbados, or other areas where wealthy and fashion-conscious English or Europeans were building and outfitting homes.

Early scholarship suggested that the Lee and Van Rensselaer papers were perhaps created by John Baptist Jackson (mentioned on page 20), who was known to have produced wallpapers with serpentine floral or arabesque framing devices around smaller designs as well as larger scenes that sometimes simulated engravings. However, those papers were printed with inks based in "oyl," and a later biographer pointed out that Jackson's business venture foundered in 1756, before the Lee Mansion was built.[55]

ONE OF THE PANELS in the corner of a room in the Lee Mansion (the hall chamber) resembles the carved pendant drops on the best parlor chimney-breast. It was hung upside-down (note the swag hanging upward from the bow at the bottom)—either by mistake, or perhaps by intent by a local laborer expressing some type of umbrage, perhaps at Lee's extravagant wealth or, conceivably, demands for a high speed of installation, as often occurs today. *MMHS*

At the papers' destination, local paper-hangers installed the strips of paper onto the walls of a home, generally using animal-based hide glues, or a paste of flour and water for lighter papers, overlapping the vertical seams. Given the large volume of wallpaper imported into the American colonies in the mid-1700s, and Marblehead's prosperity at that time, there certainly would have been paper-hangers and retailers of wallpaper in Marblehead.[56] Uncommon papers like these murals would have been specially ordered from England, generally through a gentleman merchant's agent or factor there.

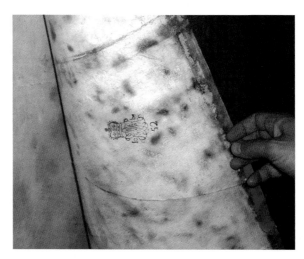

ON THE BACKS OF EACH SHEET OF PAPER was a stamped mark—a cipher with an intertwined GR for "George Rex" underneath a crown and above a letter or number that denoted a particular time period for an English excise tax. The stamps, which are seen on the backs of printed papers as well, indicated that the required tax had been paid to the Crown by the *manufacturer*, not by the purchaser. Several were found on the Lee Mansion and Van Rensselaer papers during conservation. The wallpaper tax began in 1712 and has nothing to do with the hated "Stamp Act," the first of several taxes imposed on colonial Americans that sparked widespread protest in 1765.[57] *MMHS, Photos by T. K. McClintock, Northeast Document Conservation Center, North Andover, MA*

PAINTED MURAL PAPERS IN THE LEE MANSION ROOMS

EIGHT FEET ACROSS, the main staircase was surrounded by mural papers that originally also covered the walls in the lower entry hall above the mahogany wainscot (see photo pages 72-73), in addition to their current considerable expanse on the second floor. *MMHS*

STAIR-HALL

The painted wallpapers along the main staircase are resplendent, especially as they extend into the spacious upper stair-hall and two large front rooms. They originally covered the entire central lower entry hall as well—just as in the two Albany houses that had them and the one whose occupant, the New Jersey governor, had petitioned to have them. However, the bank that owned the Lee Mansion from 1804 to 1904 found it necessary to remove the papers from the lower entry hall in 1895.[58] Not long after the mansion's purchase by the historical society in 1909, scrollwork frames similar to those on the original wallpapers were apparently painted directly on the walls of the first-floor central entry;[59] fifty years later, in 1966, French wall coverings painted with rococo flourishes around a rectangle, but with no scenes, were installed to suggest the former presence of scenic wallpapers, rather than to detract from the actual originals by replicating them downstairs.[60]

THE MURAL PAPERS extend behind the large portraits of the Lees, where late-nineteenth-century copies of the originals hang today. *Photo by Frank Cousins, ca. 1891, published as a postcard by the Essex Institute in Salem, MA, MMHS and Author's Collection*

ON THE STAIR LANDING, surrounded on all sides by the large scenic murals, a grand Palladian effect is created by tall fluted pilasters with scrolled capitals at either side of the immense arched or "compass" or "round-headed" window,[61] while the two full-size Lee portraits embody the aura of majesty the entire scene would have conveyed. *MMHS, Photo by D. Bruce Greenwald*

Second Floor

The vast expanse of glorious hand-painted scenic mural papers extends into a spacious upper salon that would have been a grand entertaining area sometimes called a "saloon"[62] at that time. Its splendor would have dazzled, and still does today.

The scenic wallpapers continued into two large and sumptuously appointed front chambers (their doors visible flanking the windows, below) that were as elegant as the parlors below them.

BELOW THE SCENIC MURAL PAPERS, gleaming mahogany wainscoting extends throughout both the upper and lower stair-halls. *MMHS*

IN THE LARGE PUBLIC AREAS of the house, which were elegant spaces for entertaining, scenes of Roman ruins were expressions of grandeur that proclaimed their owner's prestige as well as his cultural sensibilities and social aspirations. *MMHS*

THIS SPACIOUS UPPER RECEPTION AREA was among the most monumental and sumptuous interior spaces in colonial America. The woodwork in this upper realm is currently painted in the mansion's original muted tones of ochre yellow that at once complement and enhance the *grisaille* mural papers. *MMHS, Photo by Rick Ashley*

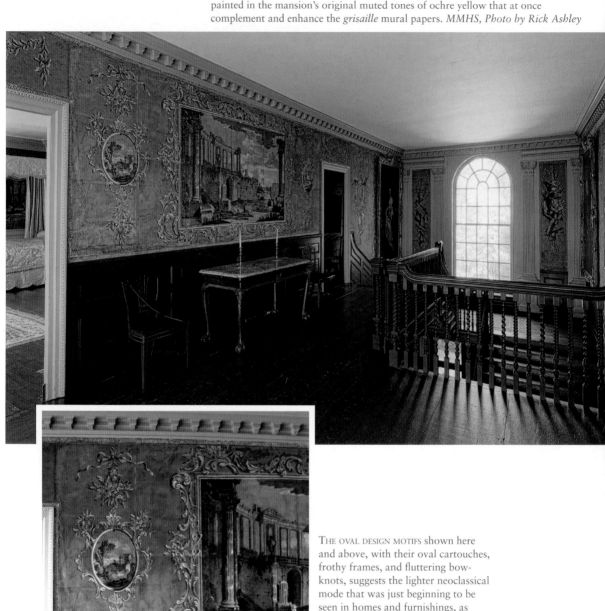

THE OVAL DESIGN MOTIFS shown here and above, with their oval cartouches, frothy frames, and fluttering bow-knots, suggests the lighter neoclassical mode that was just beginning to be seen in homes and furnishings, as does much of the imagery on the Van Rensselaer papers. *MMHS*

HALL CHAMBER

A large, stately room above the dining parlor or "hall"[63] was most likely for entertaining and for important guests. There, they could have withdrawn after dinner for a round of punch or a game of cards, with talk of trade or the state of affairs in the province, port or Madeira flowing or punch ladled from a large ceramic bowl, or stayed the night if they had traveled from some distance away. As a bedroom above the parlor or "hall" below, it would have been referred to as the "hall chamber." All four walls are extravagantly covered by scenes of ruins and large Roman armorial emblems.

THE WALLPAPER SCENES in a large second-floor front room continue the grand Roman themes seen in the adjacent upper stair-hall, suggesting its public nature as a formal multipurpose space, for dining or sleeping or entertaining in high-level style with distinguished guests.[64] *MMHS*

THE ROOM IS FURNISHED in yellow silk damask, based on the colonel's household inventory taken a year after his death.[65] Window curtains listed en suite with the other textiles were most likely of the festoon type that were drawn upwards, probably with no upper valances that would have hidden the decorative projecting woodwork molding above the windows. The white architrave around the fireplace is imported marble. *MMHS*

RARE CARPETING LISTED ON THE INVENTORY—possibly even wall-to-wall, which was highly unusual in private homes at this time, but possible given Lee's great wealth—was likely in this room; this reproduction from a documented 1758 design shows the close associations between wallpaper and carpet patterns, as well as with wallpapers and other upholstery and curtain fabrics.[66] *Sample on loan to the MMHS by John Buscemi, Belfry Historic Consultants LLC, Lynn, Massachusetts*

PARLOR CHAMBER

In a smaller, more informal chamber at the front of the house, the walls are adorned with romanticized scenes based on French paintings. Three of the four relate directly to Lee's business of fishing and shipping. The room's location and its high level of decorative finish—including English polychrome ceramic tiles and tall fluted pilasters with capitals in the Ionic order flanking the chimney-breast—combined with the wallpaper scenes and ornaments that all relate to fishing and shipping, suggest that it was a room for use by Colonel Lee.[67] A handwritten inscription on the back of one of the mural panels identifies the room as the "Parlor Chamber," meaning a bedroom above the parlor (see photo page 36).

THE PAINTED SCENIC PAPERS make this room a very high-caliber space, suitable for a gentleman of Lee's great wealth and high status. The ceramic tiles around the fireplace are rare multicolored or "polychrome" tiles by Sadler and Greene of Liverpool, England, and are one of only three sets in Massachusetts.[68] They originally extended down the right sides of the fireplace. The woodwork is painted its original soft green hue.[69] *MMHS*

ORNAMENTING THE WALLS on either side of the front windows are painted clusters of fishing accoutrements. *MMHS, Photo by D. Bruce Greenwald*

THE LARGE SCENES are based on engravings of French paintings by Joseph Vernet (1714–89); the engravers for the scenes have been identified as Jean Jacques LeVeau (1729–85) and a French engraver who, like few others, appears to have been a woman, Anne-Philibert Coulet (born 1736).[70] *MMHS*

BETWEEN THE WINDOWS is Neptune, the god of the sea that brought Lee his wealth. The border is a later Gothic-style replacement from the 1800s. Above him, note the shell and a grotto-esque face at the top. The ceramic figures in a neoclassical style are pearlware, English, ca. 1780–1820, and represent the sea god Neptune (called Poseidon in Greek) and women from classical literature mourning beside a funerary urn on a pedestal. *MMHS*

THE BLOCK-PRINTED WALLPAPERS

The superb scenic painted mural papers were not the only wallpapers originally in the Lee Mansion. They were actually part of an extensive decorative plan that would have included other stylish wallpaper patterns as well, along with English textiles in a variety of colors and types, and six English carpets—an unusually large number for that time in America. It appears that seven different patterns of block-printed English papers graced the walls of several other rooms on all three floors of the house.

Though only one of the patterns still remains on the walls, large pieces of six of those seven patterns, each two by three feet, are preserved in the Marblehead Museum archives, along with three different borders—one stencil and two printed.[71] Removed at an unknown date, the panels and borders were saved as samples and framed for display early in the 1900s. Attempts to determine their specific original locations throughout the house have so far not yielded answers.[72] Fragments of a seventh pattern and a stencil border, the same as one used with another pattern, but in a different colorway, are in the Smithsonian, Cooper-Hewitt, National Design Museum, in New York City.[73]

Many of the better early American homes had printed wallpapers after about 1750, and examples exist in a handful of historic houses and in three principal museum collections, all block-printed or stenciled and printed. But papers from the 1700s survive primarily in fragments. Few pieces are as large as these, and seldom on either side of the ocean do so many survive from one house.[74] And most early wallpaper pieces date from after the Revolution, when wallpapers first began to be printed in America, were imported in greater volume from England, and were also imported from France.

Representing a range of styles popular at that time, these six printed patterns comprise one of the largest collections of mid-eighteenth-century wallpapers in America, especially together with their four different borders, which are particularly rare. Those include a mock-flock border that matched its sidewall pattern, a floral border that was apparently used with three different sidewall patterns, a partially stenciled zigzag sprig border that accompanied two different patterns, and the egg-and-dart border of the scenic papers, which was meant to simulate three-dimensional plaster or wood carving. In the eighteenth century, both sellers and purchasers considered wallpapers to be incomplete without borders.[75]

A printed architectural pattern, as often seen along the principal staircases or in the formal rooms of better American homes such as the handsome Marblehead house shown below, was apparently not featured in the Lee Mansion. The painted mural papers with their majestic ruins would have filled that role in the Lees' house instead.[76]

GENERAL JOHN GLOVER HOUSE IN MARBLEHEAD, C.1761

FRAGMENTS OF A POPULAR TYPE of architectural pattern with arches and columns—in this case festooned with floral garlands and printed in black, white, and brown on a bright blue ground—survive from the fine home of a merchant and innkeeper who succeeded Lee as colonel of the militia, John Glover, near Marblehead's waterfront.[77] The pieces are part of the comprehensive wallpaper collection of Historic New England. *Gift of Mr. & Mrs. G. Frank Cram (1967.28), Courtesy of Historic New England*

Five of the printed Lee patterns were floral, in a variety of colors and patterns, but all in a vibrant and asymmetrical rococo mode with organic flourishes and flowers and trailing vines. Several patterns incorporated pinks and greens, with black or crimson highlights, though the colors have faded from their once brilliant hues. The large formats of the patterns were designed for rooms in which light levels were very low.

Two floral patterns were printed on blue backgrounds that were once very bold, with white and black accents. One simulated wallpapers from the same time period that were flocked with actual wool shavings to simulate cut velvet fabric—highly popular in England in the mid-1700s even after they had already gone out of fashion in France.[78] The other may have actually been flocked, since a fragment from the Lee Mansion in the Historic New England collection appears to retain traces of wool flock on the vines[79] (see photo page 52). Printed patterns of this type without the actual wool texture were sometimes called "mock-flock" papers.

THE BLACK PRINTED
FLOWERS on this paper
were inspired by
woven silk damask
textiles, and were
meant to simulate
hand-cut velvet
fabrics. On the once-
bold blue background,
exquisitely minute
white spangles visually
suggested the actual
sparkled surfaces
created by mica flecks
on some of the best
printed wallpapers.[80]
The corresponding
blue border is one of
four borders in the
collection.[81] *MMHS
Collection, Photo by
T. K. McClintock,
Studio TKM*

LIGHTER AND MORE INFORMAL than the pattern on page 51, this blue paper featured a lighter rococo floral design with a grey diaper-weave background. It would have been appropriate for an upstairs bedchamber, and could have been hung with the other blue paper's border. The very faded background would originally have been a much bolder blue. *MMHS Collection, Photo by T. K. McClintock, Studio TKM*

A DIFFERENT PATTERN REPLICATED a cotton "chints" fabric from India, a relatively new and highly popular import. Beautifully exotic flowers spring from sinewy vines, with diminutive white blossoms scattered among them—lovely and most appropriate for a bedchamber (see dollhouse, pages 32–33). Pigment analysis in 2006 determined that the color of its faded background was Prussian blue, with flowers whose petals were originally deep red (vermillion and Prussian blue combined) around delicate and lacy white centers.[82] *MMHS Collection, Photo by T. K. McClintock, Studio TKM*

THE GREEN BACKGROUND of this delightful floral trailing vine pattern in an asymmetrical rococo spirit is overlaid with a delicate latticework printed in black. The paper may have been burnished or glazed to give it a sheen that would have made it shimmer in candlelight.[83] Note the floral border that does not directly match in color or pattern. *MMHS Collection*

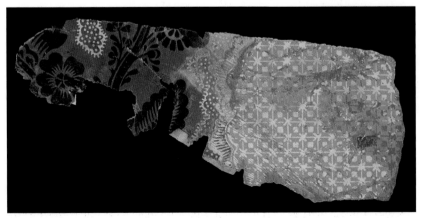

A FRAGMENT of paper from the Lee Mansion in the collection of Historic New England shows traces of wool flock on the floral vines. *Gift of Miss Lucy Brigham (1934.07) Courtesy of Historic New England*

AGAINST A PINK BACKGROUND, a fifth floral pattern had flowers printed in white, green, and black colors, apparently with the same zigzag sprig border (fragment far right) as the pattern below. It survives only in six small fragments that were donated to the Cooper-Hewitt Museum in New York City in 1938 (then the Cooper Union Museum for the Arts of Decoration).[84] *Gift of Miss Grace Lincoln Temple, (1938-82-27), Courtesy Cooper-Hewitt, National Design Museum, Smithsonian Institution/Art Resource, NY*

This pattern is not represented in the MMHS Collection.

FORMERLY WITH PINK, BLACK, AND WHITE highlights against a grey background, this pattern and its partially stenciled zigzag sprig border (fragment at upper left) served as a period prototype that has been reproduced for several mid-1700s room interpretations, including the chamber of a house at Colonial Williamsburg and a background for a display of furnishings from the same period in the Museum of Fine Arts, Boston.[85] *MMHS Collection, (detail) Photo by T. K. McClintock, Studio TKM*

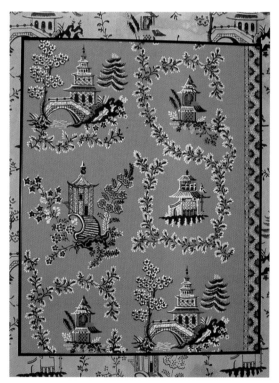

SEEN CLEARLY IN THE REPRODUCTION SHOWN HERE, this *Chinoiserie* wallpaper was stamped and partially stenciled with a stylized pattern of four different Chinese pagoda designs encircled by cherry blossom sprigs in a pink and grey color combination that was new and popular at that time. Behind it is a reproduction called "The Canton" made by the Thomas Strahan Company and installed in the Lee Mansion's side staircase and third-floor hallway in 1922.[86] *MMHS Collection, Wallpaper reproduction hand-printed by Adelphi Paper Hangings LLC*

THIS REPRODUCTION by the Thomas Strahan Company of Chelsea, Massachusetts, was installed in 1922, in areas where the original might have been, including the side entry (left) and third floor stair landing (right). *MMHS*

Two of the seven English paper patterns had Chinese motifs and imagery inspired by the period's fascination with exotic Oriental adornment, in a mode now known as *Chinoiserie*—ornamentation on luxury goods produced in England or on the European continent with specific elements from Asian arts and design.[87] Though many floral patterns reflect some of that, true *Chinoiserie* wallpaper patterns made in England or Europe in the 1700s are now rare.

One of the Lees' Chinoiserie patterns was more stylized than the other, but both were printed on grey backgrounds that had become quite fashionable. The two borders that accompanied each of them were also apparently used with three of the other floral papers, even though the patterns did not necessarily match.

A reproduction of the pink and grey *Chinoiserie* pattern currently hangs in the Lee Mansion, possibly in the areas where the original had been. It was screen-printed in the 1920s by the Thomas Strahan Company in Chelsea, Massachusetts. Waterhouse Wallhangings offered a similar screened pattern based on the original, beginning in the 1950s. Most recently, a hand-block printed version by Adelphi Paperhangings has been available in several colorways since 2001.

PEYTON RANDOLPH HOUSE IN COLONIAL WILLIAMSBURG, VA

THE REPRODUCTION pattern from the Lee Mansion original was commissioned for an interpretive installation in an upstairs chamber of the Peyton Randolph house at Colonial Williamsburg in 1999. *Photo courtesy of The Colonial Williamsburg Foundation*

WALLPAPERS WERE USUALLY PRINTED with wood blocks in a series of layers, beginning with the largest design elements and ending with the smallest highlights. A reproduction of the Lee Mansion's pink *Chinoiserie* wallpaper was printed in 1999 for the Colonial Williamsburg Foundation, on a replica wooden press that was part of an authentically based wallpaper printing operation at the Farmers' Museum in Cooperstown, NY.[88] It has been available since then through Adelphi Paper Hangings, a commercial printer that produces heritage wallpapers using historic methods.[89] *Photo courtesy of Adelphi Paper Hangings LLC*

FOR PRINTING, each one of the series of carved wooden blocks was pressed onto a piece of felt in a sieve-box or paint-box to receive the hand-mixed paint, then pressed onto a roll of paper that had already been painted with an overall background color. As today, a variety of color combinations was generally offered. This wood block is one of the four that were needed to re-create the pattern of the Lee Mansion's pink *Chinoiserie* wallpaper (in this case, along with two sets of stencils), engraved from precise drawings made from the original paper pattern. *Photo by Steve Larson, Adelphi Paper Hangings LLC*

The other *Chinoiserie* pattern was more elaborate, with engaging scenes of pagodas, cherry trees, peony flowers, and a Chinese man and boy on a pathway, printed in a very painterly manner. This is believed, to date, to be the only *Chinoiserie* paper in England or America still *in situ*.[90] It originally extended from floor to ceiling, though only the top half remains.[91] The matching border was also used with two of the other floral papers in different color palettes (see page 52, top photos, center & right).

CHINESE MOTIFS IN GREEN, BLACK, AND WHITE on a background of grey, which was a fairly newly fashionable color at that time, were accented in crimson or magenta on the peony flowers, the man's robe, and the boy's pantaloons.[92] *MMHS Collection, in situ*

THIS EXQUISITELY COMPLEX AND HIGH-STYLE PATTERN with Chinese pagodas, cherry trees, peony flowers, and a Chinese man and boy on a pathway may be the only English Chinoiserie paper still in place in America or England (detail). *MMHS Collection, in situ*

REPRODUCTION PATTERN FROM DANIEL SARGENT HOUSE, GLOUCESTER, MA 1760s

A COLOR SCHEME very similar to the border of the Lee Mansion's green *Chinoiserie* pattern can be seen in this reproduction by the Thomas Strahan Company, which was based on fragments found in the home of the Daniel Sargent family in Gloucester in 1915, when the house was torn down.[93] The Lees' side-wall paper would have had a more blue-green appearance (as determined by pigment analysis by Susan Buck of Williamsburg, Virginia). *Photo by Prudence Fish, Gloucester, MA, Courtesy of Daniel Recoder, Waterhouse Wallhangings/Thomas Strahan at the Christopher Norman Collection, New York, NY*

THE BORDER WITH THIS *Chinoiserie* pattern, printed in green and black with crimson floral accents, was also used with two of the floral sidewall patterns on page 52 (top center & right). Borders did not necessarily match in color or design the sidewall patterns they framed. *MMHS Collection, in situ, Photo by Marcia J. Hunkins*

BLOCK-PRINTED WALLPAPERS
IN LEE MANSION ROOMS

It is possible that block-printed wallpapers enhanced seven or more rooms in the Lee Mansion.

The most prominent room would have been the smaller front first-floor parlor opposite the large fully paneled dining parlor. All other areas were secondary spaces, and some even less important rooms, principally bedchambers, in the back half of the house, on the first, second, and third floors. Those included two suites of three rooms, one above the other, as well as the generous winding staircase that ascended from the family's side entry, and perhaps three or five chambers and two hallways on the third floor.

❮ IN THE SMALLER FRONT PARLOR, the mid-1700s needlework carpet from continental Europe shows a type of textile pattern that inspired wallpapers. This room likely lacked curtains, as many houses did at that time; the tall full-height window shutters featured raised panels on both faces, indicating that the backs of the shutters were meant to be seen. *MMHS, Photo by Geoffrey Gross for Great Houses of New England, Rizzoli, NY*

FAMILY PARLOR

The elegant room to the right of the entry stair-hall as one entered the mansion would have been finely accoutered with wallpapers above the paneled wooden wainscot. While it is possible that more scenic papers were here, it is more likely that the papers in this room were printed—perhaps the fashionable floral papers (see photos pages 48, 51, and this page). The room would have been used for less-formal dining or entertaining, or by the family, who would customarily have entered the house from a side entrance, also fashionably wallpapered, located behind the door to the right of the fireplace.

THE WOODWORK IN THE FRONT PARLOR was originally the same light yellow-tan "stone" color as the best dining parlor, the arched window and pilasters on the stair landing (pages 17 & 40), and the larger second-floor chamber whose sophisticated cornice molding is shown here. *MMHS, Photo by Rick Ashley*

ONE OF THE BLOCK-PRINTED WALLPAPERS will be reproduced for the room at left, and the woodwork repainted in its original color, when funding allows. *MMHS Collection*

ENGLISH CERAMIC TILES surrounding the fireplace featured delightful rococo scenes and borders, transfer-printed in black. They would have complemented either of the high-style green or blue wallpapers with black trailing floral vines with which the family's parlor was likely papered on the plaster areas (white in the photo at left). The woodwork was painted turquoise in 1940. *Author's Collection*

THE FIREBOARD from ca. 1801 in front of the fireplace was painted in oil with a scene of two-masted schooners, essential to the fishing industry and trade. The table, chair, sea captain's portrait, and the Marblehead vessels depicted in the framed pictures and on the English ceramics also date from after the Revolution. *MMHS*

THE WALLS OF WHAT WAS LIKELY Lee's business office may well have been papered. One of the two smaller rooms may have been a private office for Colonel Lee. The desk in the small office at right was made and signed by Nathan Bowen of Marblehead; it is one of several case pieces in the MMHS collection attributed to and signed by three different local cabinetmakers in the last quarter of the 1700s. *MMHS*

COUNTING OR "COMPTING" ROOM

A suite of three first-floor rooms behind the larger dining parlor was likely the office where Colonel Lee managed his shipping business. There, he could have met with the captains of his ships, and his clerks and apprentices would have kept the accounts for his complex Atlantic trade enterprise. Though the room was likely used exclusively by men, the robust woodwork may well have been complemented by wallpapers—perhaps one of the surviving floral patterns, or an eighth printed pattern, maybe with stripes, newly fashionable, or even a plain-colored paper that no longer survives. (New Jersey Governor William Franklin suggested for his "Study or Office": "A common Green Paper will do, as [a] great Part of the Wall will be covered with Books, Maps, &c.")[94]

In front of the fireplace is a fireboard (also pictured on page 13)—a wooden panel that could beautify a room while hiding the cavernous black opening of the firebox in warmer months when fires were not needed. Fireboards were often decoratively painted, but were sometimes covered with wallpapers instead. Few of either type survive. Wallpaper was also used to line books, traveling trunks, and (more often somewhat later) "band" boxes for storing hats.

BEDCHAMBER SUITE

A commodious suite of three private rooms directly above the three first floor offices would certainly have been wallpapered. It may have been used by Mrs. Lee at some point as a bedchamber, with smaller anterooms attached, emulating aristocratic couples or other well-to-do people who could enjoy and sought the luxury of separate spaces. This suite would certainly have been wallpapered, most likely with one of the block-printed floral papers, or perhaps the blue-green-hued *Chinoiserie* pattern still in the hallway just above this suite, and linked to it by a small staircase.

A DELICATE EIGHTEENTH-CENTURY Chinese wallpaper hand-drawn in pencil and watercolor was added in the 1940s to one of the small rooms that has a diminutive fireplace, which would have been especially welcome for washing in front of, or for reading in a comfortable easy chair, as shown.[95] *MMHS*

THE TWO SMALL ROOMS opening off the principal bedchamber would have been called "closets" in the eighteenth century, meaning a small private space, for dressing or simply as a comfortable private retreat. *MMHS*

THE ORIGINAL RUST-TONED TRANSFER-PRINT TILES around the fireplace would have provided a striking but complimentary color contrast to the woodwork color, which was similar to the current color, based on the original Prussian blue—a popular color choice for upstairs chambers in the American colonies in the early-to-mid-1700s.[96] *MMHS*

THE SUITE OF ROOMS, which shared a wall with the portrait of Mrs. Lee, opens to the main stair-hall on the second floor, and could access the third floor via a small staircase that, though probably somewhat altered, appears to be original. *MMHS*

A STEEP, NARROW SERVICE STAIR to the right of the fireplace unobtrusively connected this room with the third floor through the chamber above it (and probably to the kitchen below as well). The tiles around the fireplace were added in the early twentieth century. Essentially hidden from view, this room, likely for servants, is located behind the wall with Colonel Lee's portrait. *MMHS*

KITCHEN CHAMBER

On the second floor, in the rear north quadrant of the house, a large chamber above the kitchen was situated behind the wall with the portrait of Colonel Lee and the huge expanse of wallpapers immediately to its right. Completely hidden from public view, it was likely for a housekeeper and/ or other servants, or perhaps a valet to serve Colonel Lee, whose chamber may have been just across from it. Whether the kitchen chamber was wallpapered is not known. As New Jersey's Governor Franklin noted, when detailing the wallpapers he requested for the house provided for his use, the housekeeper's chamber "need not be papered" (see page 31, top right corner of map). In the end, the one in that house was, however, and that may have been the case in the Lees' mansion as well.

Even this third-floor room, perhaps a chamber for the youngest Lee children, may have been wallpapered. The door to the right of the fireplace leads to a narrow staircase that connects to the kitchen chamber below. *MMHS*

THIRD FLOOR

The mansion's full third floor was unusually large, with ceilings nearly eight feet high, and it was very finely finished for its time. The two or three principal third-floor chambers, of six large third-floor rooms, would almost certainly have been wallpapered. Though such a high level of décor on a third floor would have been unconventional for the time, the large number of printed wallpapers that appear to be from the house indicate that may have been the case.

The third-floor rooms would have accommodated the Lees' children (the eldest was at Harvard College by the time the mansion was complete) and perhaps some of the household servants, whose number and identities are unknown. Two front rooms, light and spacious but lacking fireplaces, may have housed older teenage boys from prominent families who came to learn the business of trade as apprentices in Lee's shipping operation; those rooms may not have been wallpapered.

This room is one of five commodious chambers on the third floor, and one of three with fireplaces and raised-panel chimney-breasts. All three of those rooms were most likely wallpapered. All fireplace tiles on the third floor were added early in the 1900s; the frames may simply have been plaster in these less important rooms. *MMHS*

This early-twentieth-century photograph shows the principal third-floor front bedroom papered with the green wallpaper with the black trailing vine—either eighteenth-century paper still on the wall, or more likely a ca. 1922 reproduction called "The Marblehead" by the Thomas Strahan Company of Chelsea, Massachusetts.[97] The large format of the pattern was designed for rooms in which light levels were very low in the era of candlelight. *Courtesy of the Marblehead Historical Commission*

THE EXTERIOR DOORWAY of the side entrance that the Lee family would have used was very elegant, framed by fluted pilasters below a triangular pediment.

DIRECTLY ACROSS FROM THE ENTRY DOOR, the staircase that ascended upwards to the second and third floor rooms was finely appointed with turned balusters and printed wallpaper above a raised panel wainscot. A color-correct wallpaper reproduction may enhance the Lee family entry at some point, thanks to the Society of Colonial Wars, which recognizes individuals like Colonel Lee who helped defend the American colonies before 1775. A listing on the colonel's probate inventory suggests that the first flight, which led up to what was likely his chamber, may have also had stair carpets. *MMHS*

SIDE ENTRY AND STAIRS

The third floor was accessed by a side staircase that ascended from the Lee family's entrance at the side of the house. The family would have entered through an exterior doorway with a high-style portico, atop massive outdoor granite steps that led upwards from a cobblestone drive. The interior entry was stylishly appointed, with printed wallpapers above raised panel woodwork; stair carpets between the first and second floors may have covered the segment of the staircase that led to the chamber that was likely Colonel Lee's. The wallpaper is thought to have been the simpler *Chinoiserie* pattern in the color scheme of pink and grey that was reproduced as "The Canton" and installed in those same areas in 1922.[98]

THE WALLPAPER is thought to have extended up the two flights of stairs, to the third floor, along a third-floor hallway, then up the stairs to the attic, and clear up to the cupola.[99] *MMHS*

THE DELICATE BEAUTY of this *Chinoiserie* paper seems somewhat incongruous up on a third floor, though it seems not to have been transferred there. It originally extended from floor to ceiling. *MMHS*

"*The ancient wallpaper fragments are as delicate as butterfly wings now, but they were once a backdrop to life as it was played out through the ages. I can envisage how the wallpaper would have gleamed by candlelight and brightened a dark room through the Winter months with its images of Summer flowers making the quiet walls dance and seem alive with foliage most fanciful, in hues once bright and cheery, though now dim and faded into the depths of time.*"

The "Gentle Author" of Spitalfields Life
http://spitalfieldslife.com

THIRD-FLOOR HALLWAY

This wallpaper with delightful Chinese imagery is thought to be the only English block-printed paper with Chinese scenes in its original home—not only in America, but in England as well—though that noteworthy distinction has always been eclipsed by the more famous scenic mural papers.

ALTHOUGH THE REASON for the high-style pattern's apparent 1760s installation in this third-floor area is perplexing, the hallway served a bedchamber that was likely occupied by Colonel Lee's eldest son, who would have been expected to be his eventual heir. An adjacent chamber was perhaps used by the Lees' eldest daughter, or maybe all three girls, as they approached and spent their teenage years in the mansion. *MMHS*

Epilogue
THE END OF THE LEE FAMILY IN THEIR MANSION

The Lee family was fated to live in their grand residence for less than a decade, before the clouds of rebellion gathered, then burst into storm as the Revolution, sweeping away the prosperity of both Marblehead and the Lees and so many other families in their town.

From the moment the Lees' grand residence began to rise in the mid-1760s, after the end of a seven-year global conflict between England and France[100] that drained British coffers, taxes were levied on Americans arbitrarily, without colonial representation in Parliament.

Marblehead's Revolutionary regiment was one of only a few comprised of men and boys almost entirely from one town—nearly six hundred men from their then-large community of just over nine hundred families—a very high proportion. The regiment provided vital service to General George Washington's Continental Army in several crucial battles in 1776 under its new leader, Colonel John Glover of Marblehead, promoted from his rank of major after Colonel Lee's death. The regiment gained fame for orchestrating and carrying out the heroic crossing of the ice-choked Delaware River on Christmas night in lashing sleet, fighting in the successful battle in Trenton, and ferrying the entire army and prisoners back across the river. The Marblehead Regiment disbanded at the end of December 1776, and Glover was promoted to general the following February.

As unrest against the perceived British tyranny increased, Colonel Jeremiah Lee took the side of the Patriot cause, and became a rebel against the increasingly repressive British economic policies that many American colonists felt would soon erode their liberties and livelihoods. Along with most others in his town—and unlike several of his fellow merchants there, including his two brothers-in-law—he cast his lot with those who sought independence from Britain and the liberty of self-government, risking and ultimately sacrificing every aspect of the privileged life he had worked for a quarter of a century to build.[101]

Lee actively participated in the mounting resistance in several official capacities, as a leader of the rebel faction in his community and as an elected leader in the provincial congress that was considered to be a treasonous body by the British king and parliament. As a colonel, Lee had led Marblehead's rebel Patriot militia, but as hostilities increased, he also trained in its ranks. And as the Colonies careened toward revolution in 1774, he became a member of one of the two secret committees led by John Hancock and Samuel Adams that coordinated the rebellion and supplied arms and provisions for the rebel Patriot army for all of Massachusetts. Lee also bought much-needed gunpowder from the American providers beyond Massachusetts and

In May 1775 at age fifty-four, Colonel Jeremiah Lee lost his life to the cause of independence as a direct result of his covert actions in the months and days before the first shots of the Revolution were fired on April 19, 1775. Elected to leadership positions in his community and in the rebel (Patriot) provincial government, he represented colonial grievances to the King's agents in Boston and helped to supply the rebel militias through purchases of ammunition and supplies that were sent secretly to a number of towns outside of Boston, including Concord, where they were stockpiled for the looming conflict—all highly treasonous acts that would have resulted in his execution if he had been caught. Most daring of all, he endeavored to purchase weapons from the European continent. His efforts, however, were cut short by his sudden death that was caused by a fever contracted while evading a raiding party from the British regular army marching toward Lexington in the early morning hours before the fateful April battle that is credited as the beginning of the Revolution.[102]

MINIATURE PORTRAIT OF COLONEL JEREMIAH LEE by John Singleton Copley, ca. 1769, ivory. *MMHS Collection, Gift of Lee descendant Mrs. Mary L. Kinsman through her son Dr. Frederick J. Kinsman, 1935*

sought to purchase weapons from the European continent for the impending rebellion through his Basque trading agent in the port of Bilbao, Spain—a highly illegal act in Britain's eyes on several levels.[103]

The revolution that created the American nation brought devastating loss of lives and property in Marblehead, including the great Lee family.

In the end, Colonel Lee and his heirs were victims of the cause that he and so many others fought to achieve. In early May of 1775, at age fifty-four, just ten weeks after his eldest daughter's marriage on the last day of February,[104] Lee met a premature and tragic end as the first patriot leader to die for his country's independence. Considered a rebel insurgent in the eyes of the British officials, he contracted a fever while evading a raiding party from the British regular army marching toward Lexington on that fateful April morning, when the first shots of the war were fired.

Few people realize the extent of Colonel Lee's covert endeavors, as they were of necessity conducted in secret, so only tantalizing bits of evidence survive to provide a glimpse into the grave risks Colonel Lee took. Nearly all records of his involvement disappeared, as did those of his entire business and his life. Later, he was not written into the Patriot story told in so many history books.

But the Lee family's grand mansion remains, attesting to how much they stood to lose, and representing the sacrifices Colonel Lee and so many others made for American independence.

And in it, the remarkable painted wallpapers present as glorious a vision as they did when the Lees first set foot in their palatial new surroundings two and a half centuries ago.

Lee Mansion History after 1775 and Preservation History

After Colonel Lee's Death 1775–1803

In spring 1775, as the Revolution began and Colonel Lee died so suddenly due to his presence near Lexington the morning of the fateful battle, life for his family and for Marblehead changed almost in an instant.

After prosperity that was followed by commitment to a perilous and uncertain but essential national cause, the story of Lee's family and Marblehead during the Revolution and afterward is one of grave sadness, courage, perseverance, and loss, both economic and personal, before eventual revival and renewed vitality a half-century later.

But in one of the many ironies of history, the economic misfortune that afflicted Marblehead during and after the Revolution ultimately preserved the Lee Mansion and so many of the town's early homes and buildings—nearly 300 built before the Revolution and more than 800 before 1840.

The social and economic hardships preserved not only the buildings and the Lee Mansion but its interiors and wallpapers as well. For after Colonel Lee's death in 1775, the great mansion was never again occupied by individual resident owners who would have made changes to the structure or its interior decorations as styles changed and tastes evolved. It has never been heated, and no plumbing or mechanical systems were ever introduced into the structure.

The Lees' mansion may not have been actively lived in by the financially struggling family—one of so many in their town—between 1775, when Lee so suddenly lost his life, and 1785, when the house transferred out of the family after the death of Lee's eldest son and his only apparent male heir that same year, two years after the Revolution ended.[105] With huge spaces that were so cold in winter, and without the staff to support the upkeep of so large a house—let alone threats from a British warship to burn the town, causing many residents to flee—Mrs. Lee and her two teenage daughters and a younger son apparently lived with the eldest married daughter in Newburyport and then Newbury.[106]

From 1785 to 1804, the mansion was owned by two wealthy out-of-town merchants who held the mortgage (one for just a year in 1786) but who did not inhabit the house or alter its interiors by converting it to apartments or other uses. It did not become a tenement, hospital, country club, or school, as happened to so many large colonial homes, nor did it suffer a fire or urban renewal or other misfortune.

Marblehead Bank 1804–1904 (Marblehead National Bank after 1860s)

This image from an 1850 survey map shows the Lee Mansion as it would have looked until the mid-1800s, when the original rooftop balustrade was removed and a cast-iron fence in the Gothic Revival style was added in front of the mansion, which served as a commercial office building for a full century through the 1800s. *Published by Henry McIntyre, 1850, MMHS and Collection of Vincent McGrath*

In 1804, the mansion was purchased by a bank founded that year as the town's first, and an early bank in the new United States.

The bank trustees proved to be prudent stewards for a full century, caring for the house well and making few noticeable changes. A marine insurance company and an attorney occupied rooms on the second floor. For years in the mid-1800s, the kitchen, the room above it, and most of the third floor where printed wallpaper did not survive served as living space for the family of the bank's resident "cashier" or manager. And the smaller front room, whose original wallpapers are unknown but which certainly had them, was their parlor until 1871, when a satellite savings bank was formed within that space after the American banking system was nationalized following the Civil War.[107] Where the one original *Chinoiserie* paper remains in the western hallway, two third-floor chambers were meeting rooms for gentlemen in the town's two political parties during the 1800s.

Remarkably, all of the painted wallpapers were kept in place for nearly the entire century of the bank's ownership. While fiscally conservative, the bank directors maintained the mansion prudently. They must also have been aware of the mural papers' importance since those irreplaceable papers were not taken down—until 1895 when the wallpapers in the lower entry hall, the office building's public reception area, had to be removed because of increasing "vandalism" by visitors, as reported in the local newspaper.[108]

By the late 1800s, Marblehead had become a seaside resort—"the yachting capital of the world"— and the extraordinary scenic papers had become a popular attraction for the many summer visitors who flocked to the seacoast town with its pleasant summer breezes. That, however, was nearly the papers' demise, as many people came specifically to see the famous "painted papers" and apparently spirited away pieces for souvenirs.[109]

The bank closed in 1904, a century after it began, and rumors circulated that the mansion's superb interiors would be removed and sold at auction.

For a full century through the 1800s, the Lee Mansion was a bank and commercial office building, with bank operations in the first-floor rooms to the left, and the offices of a marine insurance company, vital in a maritime town, in a suite of four rooms above it. In 1871, a satellite savings bank opened in the smaller first-floor front parlor, below the second-floor office of a local attorney. (Note the two signs for the two banks above the two front rooms.) *Photo by unknown photographer, after 1871, MMHS Collection*

The mansion was rescued in 1909 through its purchase by the Marblehead Historical Society. The group had been founded in 1898 to collect artifacts relating to the town's heritage, and was seeking a space for its headquarters. Donations and fund-raising events brought the $5,000 needed to purchase the building and thereby keep it intact. Public tours were offered the very first year. The mansion has been open seasonally and maintained prudently ever since.

IN THE 1800s, neither the scenic murals nor the green *Chinoiserie* wallpapers on the third floor, where gentlemen's meetings were held, were immune to damage from souvenir-taking. Someone, in a manner quite cheeky, penciled the following words onto the plaster, under a section that was patched at some point: *"Notice—Some vandal cut this / figure out and carried it off. / Be kind enough not to follow his or her mean example."*[110] *MMHS, Photo by T.K. McClintock, Studio TKM*

THE SCENIC WALLPAPERS once filled the lower stair-hall, but were removed in 1895 because of increasing "vandalism" by people visiting the bank in the 1800s to see the famous "painted papers." Mural scenes reminiscent of the papers were apparently painted at some point; after those had aged, special French papers with scrollwork frames but no scenes were installed in 1966 to evoke a sense of the former presence of paper murals in that vast area. *Photo by Frank Cousins, 1891, MMHS Collection*

The Marblehead Historical Society has owned, maintained, and preserved the Lee Mansion for more than a century. The word "Museum" was added to its name in 2003. *Photos by Judy Anderson, Lee Mansion curator and preservation project grant-writer 2001 through 2009, the mansion's centennial year of ownership by the MMHS*

THE MARBLEHEAD MUSEUM & HISTORICAL SOCIETY's first century of Lee Mansion ownership and preservation was celebrated in 2009, after several major preservation projects and just before this booklet was written.

Throughout that century, the nationally significant Lee Mansion and its unparalleled wallpapers have been maintained wisely and conservatively by the small local historical association, always with a limited budget and minimal staff (principally one person through 1992 and never really more than four after that, as the museum grew), as in many historical and cultural organizations like it, and many enthusiastic volunteers. The museum is also responsible for a large collection of more than 60,000 artifacts, archives, and high-quality decorative arts; changing exhibits in a separate building with offices, galleries, and the archival collection; archives research service; collections management; and maintenance of that second building.

In 1998, the Marblehead Historical Society's centennial year, a modern building across the street from the Lee Mansion was purchased to accommodate the Society's growing collections, year-round operations, and changing exhibits, further protecting the Mansion and its wallpapers.

In the mid-1970s, mid-1980s, and especially after 2000, federal government grants and matching grants from private foundations enabled several major conservation endeavors to be completed for various aspects of the Lee Mansion structure and the first two of three phases of conservation for the scenic papers. Local contributions supported much of the first four years of wallpaper conservation in the 1980s, as well as other building preservation in the last half of the 1990s. Though some significant needs remain for the house and its wallpapers, including the third and largest phase of wallpaper conservation, careful ongoing stewardship has preserved both the scenic murals and the building well.

The Marblehead Museum & Historical Society bears a challenging responsibility, especially for an organization whose founding and ongoing mission was not exclusively the Lee Mansion nor its remarkable wallpapers, but was, and still is, the preservation, education, and celebration of a broad spectrum of Marblehead's four hundred years of history.

Operations for both the museum and the Lee Mansion are supported by contributions from many individuals, with no municipal funding.

The more these exceptional wallpapers are known, the more they will be visited and appreciated—which will, in turn, help to preserve these unique and magnificent artworks well into the future.

CONSERVATION OF THE SCENIC MURAL PAPERS by skilled experts, both on-site in the mansion and in a studio, has been diligent and exacting. More work is still needed and awaits funding. *Photo by T.K. McClintock, Studio TKM*

CONCLUSION

"The Jeremiah Lee Mansion is a national treasure! With extraordinary original wallpapers and exceptional carved architectural details, it ranks among the most important expressions of high-style eighteenth-century interior decoration to survive in North America."

Dean Lahikainen
Carolyn and Peter Lynch Curator of American Decorative Art,
Peabody Essex Museum, Salem, MA

The Lee Mansion's hand-painted mural papers—the crowning splendor of this incomparable house—are a significant part of the heritage of one of the first independent nations in the world, which Marblehead's Colonel Jeremiah Lee—the peerless businessman, enigmatic patriot, and luminary in his day who ordered and commissioned them—helped to bring about in a fleeting but heroic way.

The papers have witnessed colonial America's commercial prosperity, rise to rebellion, the losses of revolution, and the independence and growth of the United States. After their inception at the nexus of colonial ambition, taste, and financial ability, followed by adversity, intermittent recovery, and their unlikely survival through both, fate has kept them in excellent condition—thanks to fortunate stewardship, local generosity, and federal government grants. With care, they can remain for centuries to come as one of the most dramatic and spectacular interior spaces from the time of the birth of the United States, which Colonel Lee helped to launch but never lived to see.

The importance of these fragile artifacts is of national magnitude, and their care is of merit to the entire country as a unique and splendid legacy from the time of America's independence, for which Colonel Lee and so many others sacrificed and paid the ultimate price. Their extraordinary survival is somewhat short of miraculous, and their continued preservation is of vital consequence that reaches far beyond the borders of Marblehead, where the Lees' grand residence and its distinctive embellishments would have dazzled in the pre-Revolutionary metropolis.

PHOTO BY Geoffrey Gross for Great Houses of New England, *Rizzoli Publishers Courtesy MMHS*

Appendix A

Wallpaper Preservation

Preserving these rare early scenic mural papers is a challenging responsibility for the small local historical association that owns the Lee Mansion. The Marblehead Museum & Historical Society receives no municipal or state funding and currently operates with a staff of four people for two buildings and a collection of more than 60,000 artifacts, including a local history and genealogy archive and an outstanding collection of decorative arts on view in changing exhibits in the museum galleries and on permanent display in the Lee Mansion.

In addition to their extreme rarity, the wallpapers are of course exceedingly fragile. Their linen content and the lack of damaging heat in the mansion have helped to preserve them over two-and-a-half centuries. They were further protected by the remarkable good fortune that the house was never owned by a family or a series of private owners who would have made decorative renovations as styles changed, but was instead owned for a century by a conservative and conscientious bank until acquired by the historical society, which had been established in 1898, just a decade before its fortuitous purchase of the mansion in 1909.

Soon after the historical society assumed stewardship of the house, some of the papers were temporarily removed from the walls so that repairs could be made by a Marblehead artisan, Thomas Pitman. He wrote pencil inscriptions on the plaster in at least two rooms documenting the date of his work "when the Historical Society came in possession of the Building." The murals were also "re-touched" around 1929 (a year after the Metropolitan Museum's mural papers were donated and repaired prior to their installation in the American Wing) by Marblehead artist Marion Martin Brown and William Young, who later became a conservator at the Museum of Fine Arts in Boston.

Afterwards, in 1930–31, large glass panels were installed over all of the papers that had not been removed by the bank in 1895, to protect them and keep them in place.[111] Funding for that was the first of several preservation, refurbishment, and redecorating projects through the 1940s that were prompted, directed, and paid for by Mrs. Louise DuPont Crowninshield, a connoisseur of historic furnishings and interiors and an advocate for historic house preservation. She had a summer home at the end of the Marblehead peninsula for many years until her death in 1958, and contributed many fine pieces of decorative arts over those years as well.

Those early preservation efforts mitigated the destructive influences of time over more than two centuries, and helped to keep the painted mural papers intact until significant funding was raised for professional conservation sixty and eighty years later.

Essential, exacting, and painstaking conservation work was performed in 1986–9 and 2005–6 by teams of experts using state-of-the-art techniques. Both project phases were led by wallpaper conservation specialist T. K. McClintock, first through the Northeast Document Conservation Center in Andover, Massachusetts, and then as his own firm, Studio TKM. Over six collective years, the wallpapers were conserved through critical preservation measures that cleaned and repaired them. Before re-attaching them to the walls, both the original plaster walls and the eighteenth-century papers were lined with special non-tearing modern paper, with fabric installed between the two as a buffer to protect the fragile papers, which respond to the environment differently than the original plaster walls, subjecting them to ongoing stress. In addition to special contributions from local individuals for the treatment in the late 1980s, much of the conservation work in all six years was supported by grants[112] (see next page).

The wallpapers on the large walls of the expansive central stair-hall still require further conservation treatment within the next decade or so.

Principal Lee Mansion Wallpaper Conservation:

LARGE GLASS PANELS installed in 1929–31 held all the remaining
original painted papers in place until comprehensive conservation
of the papers in all three areas, one room per year, in 1986–89.
Photo by Samuel Chamberlain, ca. 1940, MMHS Collection

1909 Removal of some of the second-floor
papers for repairs by a Marblehead artist,
Thomas Pitman, followed by re-attachment
onto the original plaster walls. That artist
had also apparently been hired by the bank to
paint murals resembling the wallpapers directly
onto the walls of the first-floor entry hall soon
after the eighteenth-century wallpapers were
removed in 1895.

1929–30 Repairs and some over-painting
(over-painting was also done in the 1800s) by
Marblehead artist Marion Brown and an art
conservator, William Young, who later worked
at the Museum of Fine Arts in Boston. That
work was followed by the installation of large
glass panels over all the scenic wallpapers to
keep them in place.
*Preservation work was funded by Mrs.
Louise DuPont Crowninshield.*

1986–90 (fund-raising 1986–91)
Treatment by a conservation team from the
Northeast Document Conservation Center in
Andover, Massachusetts, led by T. K. McClintock, who became the principal of Studio TKM during
the project. A full condition assessment and treatment proposal in 1986 followed by removal, cleaning,
conservation, and lining of the papers and the walls in the smaller front second-floor room in 1986–87.
Full repairs with the wallpapers in place in the larger front second-floor chamber in 1988. Extensive
meticulous repairs, re-adhering, and stabilization in the stair-hall in 1989–90, also in place. Over-
painting from the nineteenth and early twentieth centuries was removed, and old repairs were remedied
or improved upon. Comprehensive treatment report for entire four-year project.
*Conservation was funded by grants from the Institute of Museum Services, a federal agency, matched by
the Fidelity Foundation and several smaller grants, as well as many local individual donations.*

2005–06 Full removal, cleaning, and conservation of the printed *Chinoiserie* wallpapers on the
third floor. The same treatment was done on four panels of the painted mural papers at the front of
the upper stair-hall, as a pilot project for future work still needed throughout the stair-hall.
*Conservation work was funded through a federal Save America's Treasures grant administered by
the National Endowment for the Arts, with matching funding from the Getty Grant Program of the
J. Paul Getty Foundation near Los Angeles, California.*

THE PAPERS WERE REMOVED from the original plaster walls with scalpels and steam before treatment in the studio. *MMHS*

THE PAPERS were moistened and gently cleaned on a suction table. *Photo by T. K. McClintock, Studio TKM*

CONSERVATION STILL NEEDED:

ca. 2015 ? Full removal, cleaning, and conservation of the rest of the mural papers in the stair-hall, including lining the walls and the wallpapers with Japanese paper and adding fabric between the papers and the plaster walls as a buffer before re-installation, as done in the 2005–06 pilot project.

That additional conservation is the last of three phases of highly specialized conservation work that will ensure the wallpapers' continued preservation. Funding sources are unknown and have yet to be sought.

For additional images of the wallpaper and other conservation, see http://marbleheadmuseum.org/ Conservation_Wallpaper.html.

SOME OF THE PAPERS were treated in place (hall chamber in 1987–88 and stair-hall in 1989–90), and others were removed for treatment in the studio (parlor chamber in 1986–87, third-floor *Chinoiserie* papers in 2005–6, and pilot project for the stair-hall, also in 2005–6). Here, the team re-installs a conserved panel in 2006. *MMHS*

Appendix B

Woodwork Paint Analysis

The original colors of the pine woodwork in the mansion's principal rooms were determined through technical microscopic paint analysis in 1984, 1991, and 2008. The original paint colors were re-created in the upstairs rooms after the first two analyses. Repainting the first-floor front parlor, recently analyzed with the larger front parlor opposite, awaits funding.

1984   Second Floor Chamber Suite *(page 61)*

A second-floor suite of three rooms was analyzed by Morgan Philips of the Society for the Preservation of New England Antiquities (S.P.N.E.A., now called Historic New England). The current hue was painted after that, though it is now slightly more green than the original Prussian blue, a popular color for upstairs chambers in the early and mid-1700s. The baseboards were dark brown, as found in all the other rooms; baseboards were often brown, and commonly called "mop-boards" for obvious reasons.

Wallpapers: An eighteenth-century Chinese wallpaper with delicate flowering vines hand-drawn in pencil and hand-painted with watercolor was installed in one of the smaller chambers of that suite in the 1940s (provided by Lee Mansion benefactor Louise DuPont Crowninshield), but the suite currently lacks any original or reproduction printed wallpapers based on eighteenth-century originals initially in those places.

‹ In 2008, conservator and paint analyst Christine Thomson investigated the front parlor's original paint colors under the ca. 1852 *faux-bois* paint that simulates oak graining, and found it to be a light yellowish tan or "stone" color (as referred to in the 1700s), meant to suggest the limestone or other stone interiors seen in aristocratic houses in England and other countries in Europe.[113] *MMHS*

1991   Second Floor Stair-Hall and Two Front Chambers *(pages 40–47)*

In preparation for re-painting after the four-year wallpaper conservation, the second-floor stair-hall and two front chambers were analyzed and re-painted in their original soft green and yellow-tan colors, based on investigation by Kathryn Carey and Bryan Powell, also through the S.P.N.E.A. Those rooms had last been painted in 1939, in a neutral white since the original colors were not then known. The paint examination and repainting were funded through donations as part of the wallpaper conservation funding package.

Wallpapers: In all three of those rooms, the original scenic wallpapers can now be seen in relation to their original eighteenth-century woodwork colors.

2008   Two First Floor Front Parlors *(pages 17 & 58)*

To augment understanding about the mansion and its original appearance during its first decade, as seen by the first and only individual owners, the colors of the woodwork in the two first-floor front parlors were analyzed by conservator and paint specialist Christine Thomson. The analysis determined that the original woodwork color of both parlors was the same yellow-tan color as the central stair-hall and the largest second-floor front chamber. According to Thomson, a unified color scheme in a "stone"-like color such as the yellow ochre found in each of those principal spaces is consistent with what has been discovered from the original colors in the interiors of other grand American houses from that time, as they sought to emulate homes of the aristocracy in their English or other European homelands, with their stone staircases and stone or plaster walls accented by wallpapers or wall fabrics. This paint study was funded by a grant from the Cynthia Woods Mitchell Fund of the National Trust for Historic Preservation, matched by donations from several volunteer Lee Mansion guides.

Wallpapers: Only the smaller of the two front parlors would have had wallpapers during the Lee time period. It was most likely one of the ca. 1760s block-printed wallpapers found in the house, as discussed on pages 49–52. A reproduction of one of those papers will be fabricated and installed when funding allows, and the woodwork repainted in its original color.

The larger front parlor was fully paneled in pine, and had no wallpapers. It will continue to retain its rare and historic 1852 *faux-bois* paint treatment that simulated oak graining by Marblehead artist William Thompson Bartoll, which is only the second generation of paint in that room over two and a half centuries.

Future Paint Analysis

To fully understand the original decorative scheme of this nationally significant house, analysis is still needed for six or seven secondary rooms, particularly in the side entry, as funding allows.

Appendix C: Fishing & the Colonial Marblehead Economy

Fishing on the Grand Banks off Newfoundland in the North Atlantic generated prosperity for Marblehead, particularly from 1716 to 1775. The fish was caught by New England fishermen on the shallow fishing grounds or "banks" of the North Atlantic over several weeks each spring and fall, then brought back to dry on the many rocky headlands of the Marblehead peninsula. The cod that "cured" or dried the best was shipped to the Catholic countries of Spain and Portugal, a major supplier of the salt required by the fishery, where Marblehead fish commanded the highest prices. As part of the Atlantic triangle trade, products acquired in the Iberian region on exchange, generally through agents in Lisbon, Portugal, or Bilbao, Spain, were brought to England to be traded for the manufactured goods the colonists in America needed and craved—textiles, glass, brass hardware, and wallpapers—again, through agents, mainly in London, but sometimes in Bristol, Liverpool, or elsewhere. Poorly cured fish was sent to the West Indies in the Caribbean for the slave populations there. The middling-quality fish was consumed locally and traded in other North American seaports for wood products, wheat, rice, tar, or other items required for the shipping industry, and a variety of other trade goods. The North Atlantic's Grand Banks off Newfoundland were opened to safer fishing by New England fishermen by a treaty with France in 1713, increasing the catch, which helped prompt Marblehead's dramatic growth from 1716 through the 1760s.

In the mid-1700s, about thirty to forty wealthy merchants and "shoremen"[114] managed the profitable fish trade that built and furnished fine homes in the seafaring community. In multiple voyages each spring and fall throughout the 1700s and after, hundreds of Marblehead fishermen labored at the grueling, arduous, and dangerous fishing that had sustained the town since its settlement in 1629, but which claimed many lives and left many widows and orphans. (After the Revolution, there were 456 widows in a town that had been filled with 935 families.) Hundreds of tradesmen and others supported the town's commerce and business, living and working in many of the ordinary eighteenth-century dwellings that are still numerous today in Marblehead and give the town its character. Though fishing thrived again in the 1820s and '30s, the industry was crushed by the double blow of the industrialization of commercial fishing and a violent gale in 1846—a "perfect storm" that claimed half the town's fishing fleet and the lives of 65 men and boys, leaving 53 widows and 144 fatherless children. Shoemaking became the staple of the economy for many decades before and after the Civil War. But after 1775 and the Revolution's economic devastation, Marblehead never again enjoyed the profits that built the Lee Mansion and so many other fine colonial homes that still stand proudly in the historic downtown—nearly 300 of the 519 homes in Marblehead in 1765.

Appendix D

Wallpaper Image Sources

The scenic images on the mural papers painted free hand by the artisans or "stainers" in the wallpaper manufactory primarily depict classical visions of a noble and heroic past, or representational scenes in landscape settings. Executed in shades of grey, black, and white called *grisaille*, they were meant to suggest engraved prints popular for collecting, placed in albums, or covering a wall. Design motifs called "trophys" or "tripolys" filled smaller spaces and provided visual accents on the walls.

THE SCENIC PANELS and decorative and armorial emblems of the mural papers were derived from eighteenth-century English and European engravings based on paintings by Italian and French artists. *MMHS, Photo by T. K. McClintock, Studio TKM, after conservation*

The imagery was based on European oil paintings (French or Italian) and emblematic designs rich with visual symbolism, used as sources for ornamental plaster or wood carving, as reproduced by engravers, primarily in England, France, or The Netherlands (The "Low Countries"—Holland and Flanders, essentially today's Belgium). For the elaborate rococo *trompe l'oeil* scrollwork frames painted around all of the scenic panels, with their richly sculptural two-dimensional *rocaille* shells, asymmetrical cartouches, and c-scroll flourishes, design sources were plentiful, and too generic to ascertain specific sources.

Some of the scenes on the mural papers and their painting or print sources have been determined, both during research for the 1932 publication (soon after the gift of an entire room to the museum's new American Wing, opened just prior to the donation), and in the 1980s, during conservation of those papers as well as of three rooms of Marblehead's Jeremiah Lee Mansion papers still *in situ* (by different conservators). That information is not included due to space limitations. Some of the imagery may have blended a variety of ornamental designs, precluding specific identification; other print sources remain undetermined, warranting further research.

In the Lee family's residence, the noble aura of the grand classical ruins and the abundance of military visual imagery befit Colonel Lee's stature and title, the fishing themes relate to the source of his wealth, the rococo flourishes and pastoral emblems speak to the family's enlightened sensibilities, and the music-themed trophy near the informal parlor suggests feminine cultural accomplishments, and the architecture symbols at the crowning height on the crest of the staircase embody the essence of the Lees' majestically classical mansion.

WALLPAPER	PAGE	SUBJECT MATTER	SOURCE IMAGE ARTIST	ENGRAVER

MAIN STAIRCASE

WALLPAPER	PAGE	SUBJECT MATTER	SOURCE IMAGE ARTIST	ENGRAVER
1 scrollwork triangle	11	rococo flourishes	unidentified	unidentified
1 trophy	39	military attributes	unidentified	unidentified

STAIRCASE LANDING

WALLPAPER	PAGE	SUBJECT MATTER	SOURCE IMAGE ARTIST	ENGRAVER
2 scenic panels	40	Roman ruins	Giovanni Paolo Pannini	J.S. Müller & T. Vivares
covered by portraits		*1 illustrated in Met article*	1691–1765 Italy	(see next room below)
1 trophy panel	7,41	classical architecture	Réné Charpentier	Jacques Gabriel Huquier
by Mrs. Lee portrait		*compass, square & paper*	1680–1723 France	1695–1772 France
2 trophy panels	4,10,11	classical armor	Jean Charles Delafosse	Pierre Francois Tardieu
flanking arched window		*helmets, shields, weapons*	1734–1789 France	1711–1771/4 France

UPPER STAIR-HALL

WALLPAPER	PAGE	SUBJECT MATTER	SOURCE IMAGE ARTIST	ENGRAVER
7 scenic panels [i]	3,8,19,20,	Roman ruins	Giovanni Paolo Pannini	Johann Sebastian Müller
4 along east wall length	34,38,81	*some are identifiable sites*	1691–1765 Italy	1720–80 b. Germany *
1 large west wall center	10,23,41,42			& Thomas Vivares
1 west wall south front	78,84		*worked in England*	1709–80 b. France *
2 north, behind portraits	*40, Met p.87*			
2 oval trophys	23,41	landscape vignettes	unidentified	unidentified
1 large trophy panel	7	classical military	unidentified	unidentified
1 smaller trophy	84	classical military	unidentified	unidentified
4 trophy panels	20,22	agrarian implements	unidentified	unidentified
1 over-door panel	1	floral basket	unidentified	unidentified
2 over-door panels	5	floral swags	unidentified	unidentified

HALL CHAMBER (The large best bedroom above the best parlor) [a]

WALLPAPER	PAGE	SUBJECT MATTER	SOURCE IMAGE ARTIST	ENGRAVER
6 scenic panels	6,43,44,77	classical ruins	Pierre Antoine de Machy	unidentified [ii]
around room		*some are specific sites*	1723–1807 France	
2 trophy panels	21	military emblems	Jean Charles Delafosse	DeWitt Janszoon
front window wall		*armor & drum*	1734–1789 France	
1 smaller trophy	--	military emblems	Jean Charles Delafosse	unidentified
south wall west corner		*assemblage of militaria*	1734–1789 France	
1 narrow pendant	37,77	fruit & flowers	unidentified	unidentified
east corner front wall		*hung upside down*		
no over-door panel		*transom panel is wood*		

PARLOUR CHAMBER (The bedroom above the smaller front parlor) [b]

WALLPAPER	PAGE	SUBJECT MATTER	SOURCE IMAGE ARTIST	ENGRAVER
4 romantic scenes		fishing & shipping	Joseph Vernet	Jean-Jacques LeVeau
east & west walls	24,45	*fishermen hauling nets*	1714–89 France	1729–1785 France * &
east wall south	46	*ships at foot of a fortress* [iii]		Anne-Philibert Coulet
west wall south	*Met p.97*	*hauling nets by waterfall*	*many English patrons*	born 1736 France *
2 trophy panels	46	fishing theme	unidentified	unidentified
south wall, corners		*fish & fishing accoutrements*		
1 panel	47	Roman god Neptune	unidentified	unidentified
between front windows		*a bearded face above him*	*(a customary mannerist motif)*	
1 over-door panel	89	scallop shell & scrolls	unidentified	unidentified
west wall above door		*less elaborate than others*		

ENTRY STAIR-HALL   (most of the first-floor murals are no longer extant; removed in 1895)

2 over-door panels above front parlor doors	86	mannerist face on each *scrollwork around it*	probably Pannini or de Machy	unidentified
1 trophy east wall, base of stairs	39,73	musical emblems *horns, drum, bagpipes & a birdcage representing song*	unidentified	unidentified

FORMERLY IN THE ENTRY STAIR-HALL   (all design sources unidentified)

5 scenic panels east & west walls	73	classical ruins *somewhat discernible on photo*
1 trophy east wall by door to parlor	73	agrarian attributes *shovel, watering can, wicker cage, sheaf of wheat*
1 large trophy	south wall front	unknown
1 vertical garland	by front door	probably floral
1 large trophy	north wall rear, left	possibly agrarian
1 scenic panel	north wall rear, right	a shipping scene
2 scenic panels	on two rear walls	maybe shipping themes
1 over-door panel	door to office, rear	unknown

CENTER PANEL in upper stair-hall, south, after conservation. *MMHS, Photo by T.K.McClintock*

The artist identifications in the chart are from the *Metropolitan Museum Studies*, vol. IV, part one, 1932, by Edna Donnell, a curator in the museum's print department at that time, and from research by conservator T.K. McClintock and Helen Hall, formerly in the paintings department at the Museum of Fine Arts, Boston, in the 1980s, and an advisor to the first phase of the Lee Mansion wallpaper conservation project at that time.

i *Edna Donnell noted that these mural scenes were "much better drawn [painted] than the other two rooms."*

ii *Some but not all of the scenes can be attributed to de Machy. For the engravers, Donnell concluded that "the scenes are such slavish copies of foreign prints that they throw no light upon the print designers."*

iii *Two ships are "breamed" or tilted over on their sides for barnacles below the waterline to be burned, or smoked, off their hulls.*

NOTES

a The *Metropolitan Museum Studies* article used the term "hall" to refer to the stair-hall; more exact terms were established for the Lee Mansion's rooms later, by conservation investigation in the late 1980s and curatorial interpretive research in the mid-1990s.

In late colonial New England, a large parlor or principal entertaining room was often referred to as a "hall"—as when Boston's Josiah Quincy marveled at the upstairs dining parlor in a splendid home in Charleston, SC, as "the grandest hall" he had ever seen. The room into which a principal exterior front door opened would generally have been called an "entry" in New England, often a "passage" in the middle Atlantic colonies and the South, and in the New York and Pennsylvania regions, either an "entry" or a "hall," as in the Metropolitan Museum's "Hall" from the manor house of Stephen Van Rensselaer, in Albany, NY, whose mural papers were ordered "for his entry."

A large open space or high-fashion public room such as the hall chamber or the upper center stair-hall in the Lee or Schuyler mansions could also have been referred to as a "salon" or "saloon."

The large best parlor at the southwest front of the Lee Mansion would most likely have been called "the hall," with "hall chamber" referring to the large and formal bedchamber—the best one—above it. It was actually written that way on an inventory of household goods taken after Mrs. Lee's death in 1791. The long 15-page inventory for Colonel Lee, recorded in June 1776, a year after his death in May 1775, was not listed room by room, perhaps due to the difficult times of those years, just as the Revolution began and impacted New England and Marblehead so directly in its first year and a half.

b Inventories generally stated a bedroom as a "chamber" and noted the room below it as a locating adjective. In 1986–7, conservation of those wallpapers determined that the east second-floor front room was in fact called the "Parlour Chamber," based on a pencil inscription on the back of one of the paper panels from that room (see page 36).

BIBLIOGRAPHY

UNPUBLISHED RESOURCES:

"*Invoice of Sundries Sent to America*" 1761–2. Philip Schuyler Papers, New York Public Library, New York, NY. (Illustrated in *Schuyler Mansion HSR*, p.15 and discussed in Lynn, p.53–56.)

Plan of Proprietary House, c.1773 (drawn in America). Trenton, NJ: State of New Jersey archives. (illus. this book, p.31.)

Plan of Van Rensselaer hall, c.1763 (drawn in America, with notations by William Squire manufactory in London), in archives of the Metropolitan Museum of Art, New York. (Illustrated in Donnell, *Metropolitan Studies*, p.85, fig.6.)

Probate inventory of Jeremiah Lee, Esq., June 5, 1776, docket #166611. Boston: Massachusetts State Archives.

UNPUBLISHED RESOURCES – in MMHS files:

Anderson, Judy (former Lee Mansion Curator). Conservation notes, grant reports, and written summary of all Lee Mansion wallpapers.

Booth, Robert W., Jr. *Col. Jeremiah Lee of Marblehead and His Mansion House.* Unpublished manuscript, 2001, in MMHS archives.

Chamberlain, Narcissa (researcher for Marblehead Historical Society, 1970s). Typewritten notes about the Lee Mansion's painted mural papers.

Hall, Helen (an advisor to the Lee Mansion wallpaper conservation project in the 1980s, formerly in the paintings department at the MFA Boston), et al. *Case statement* for the conservation of the Lee Mansion wallpapers, 1986.

Hunt, Bette (Executive Secretary of the Historical Society 1982–1993). Oral recollections to author, 1993.

Variety of handwritten minutes, notes, and correspondence, 1898–1993.

CONSERVATION – published & unpublished:

Anderson, Judy. "Renowned Teams Conserve Wallpaper and Windows" in MMHS *Newsletter,* Summer 2006, p.2.

Heckscher, Morrison H. with Marjorie Shelley. "Architectural Preservation in the Metropolitan's American Wing: The Van Rensselaer Room and the Sullivan Staircase" in *The Preservation and Use of Artistic Cultural Heritage: Perspectives and Solutions,* May 1980, p.127–132.

McClintock, T.K. Conservation Treatment Proposal for Lee Mansion wallpaper. Studio TKM, 2003.

McClintock, T.K. Conservation Treatment Reports for Lee Mansion wallpaper. 1990 & 2007.

Northeast Document Conservation Center—3 rooms, painted papers, (1986–89), 1990.

Studio TKM—4 painted mural panels, green printed *Chinoiserie* printed papers, & individual block-printed pieces, (2005–6), 2007.

McClintock, T.K. "Conservation of Historic Wallpapers." Address for *New England Conservation Association,* September 2006.

Shelley, Marjorie. "The Conservation of the Van Rensselaer Wallpaper," Metropolitan Museum of Art, *Journal of the American Institute of Conservation,* vol. 20, 1981, p.126–138.

THE LEE MANSION AND ITS WALLPAPERS – featured & illustrated in:

Ashley, Rick (photographer). *The Jeremiah Lee Mansion: A Photographic Tour.* Marblehead, MA: MMHS, 2010.

Blackburn, Roderic (Geoffrey Gross, photographer). *Great Houses of New England.* New York: Rizzoli, 2008, p.56–65.

Chamberlain, Narcissa (Samuel Chamberlain, photographer). "The Jeremiah Lee Mansion." *The Magazine Antiques,* December 1977, p.1164–74.

Hall, Helen (Samuel Chamberlain, photographer). "The Lee Mansion, Marblehead." *Country Life Magazine,* 20 January 1972, p.144–148.

Howard, Hugh (Roger Straus, photographer). *Houses of the Founding Fathers.* New York: Workman Publishing, 2007, p.56–66.

Lambton, Lucinda (Lucinda Lambton, photographer). *Old New World,* London: HarperCollins Publishers, 2000, p.8–13.

Maurer, David (Gordon Beall, photographer). "The Jeremiah Lee Mansion." *Colonial Homes Magazine,* September 1998, p.80–85.

McAlester, Virginia & Lee (Alex McLean, photographer). *Great American Houses and Their Architectural Styles.* New York: Abbeville Press, 1994, p.20-30.

THE LEE MANSION WALLPAPERS – featured and illustrated in:

Anderson, Judy. "Historic Wallpapers in the Jeremiah Lee Mansion." *Antiques and Fine Art,* Summer/Autumn 2009, p.168–173.

Donnell, Edna. "The Van Rensselaer Painted Wall Paper." *Bulletin of the Metropolitan Museum of Art,* 1931, vol. XXVI, December, section II, p.10–16.

Donnell, Edna. "The Van Rensselaer Wall Paper and J.B. Jackson." *Metropolitan Museum Studies,* vol. IV, part I, 1932, p.76–108.

Evans, Guy. "Cultured Elegance: English 18th c. Scenic Wallpapers." *Wallpaper History Review.* London: Wallpaper History Society, 2001, p.28–30.

Frangiamore, Catherine Lynn. "Landscape Wallpaper in the Jeremiah Lee Mansion," *The Magazine Antiques,* December 1977, p.1174–79.

THE LEE MANSION WALLPAPERS – briefly referenced and illustrated in:

Heckscher, Morrison H. "Architecture" in *American Rococo, 1750–1775: Elegance in Ornament.* New York: Harry N. Abrams, 1992, p.20–21.

Kosuda-Warner, Joanne, with Elizabeth Johnson. *Landscape Wallcoverings.* London: Scala Publishers with the Cooper-Hewitt, National Design Museum, Smithsonian Institution, New York, 2001, p.26–27.

Little, Nina Fletcher. "English Engravings as Sources of New England Decoration," *Old Time New England,* vol.54, Spring 1964, p.96–105.

Lynn, Catherine. *Wallpaper in America: From the 17th Century to World War I.* New York: W.W. Norton & Co., 1980, p.38–39, 55, & 67–68.

McClelland, Nancy. *Historic Wall-Papers, from Their Inception to the Introduction of Machinery.* Philadelphia: J. B. Lippincott, 1924, p.141–150.

Nylander, Richard C. "An Ocean Apart: Imports and the Beginning of American Manufacture" in *The Papered Wall,* Lesley Hoskins, ed. London: Thames & Hudson, 1994, p.43.

Nylander, Richard, with Elizabeth Redmond and Penny Sander. *Wallpaper in New England.* Boston: Society for the Preservation of New England Antiquities, 1986, p.7 & 43.

Sanborn, Kate. *Old Time Wall Papers.* New York: E.P. Dutton & Co., 1905, plate XXI (misidentified as in Salem, MA) (*Plate LII identifies a paper from a 'set found at Marblehead' that was not in the Lee Mansion*).

THE OTHER HOUSES:

Van Rensselaer Manor:

Heckscher, Morrison and Daniel Ackermann. "Great Hall of Van Rensselaer Manor House, Albany, New York (28.143)" in *Heilbrunn Timeline of Art History*. New York: The Metropolitan Museum of Art, 2000–. http://www.metmuseum.org/toah/works-of-art/28.143.

Heckscher, Morrison H. "Architecture" in Heckscher, M. & Leslie Greene Bowman. *American Rococo, 1750-1775: Elegance in Ornament*. New York: Harry N. Abrams, 1992, p.20–21.

Peck, Amelia. "The Van Rensselaer Hall" and "The Kirtlington Park Room" in *Period Rooms in the Metropolitan Museum of Art*. New York: Harry N. Abrams, 1994, p.197–203 & p.137–146.

Schuyler Mansion:

Historic Hudson Valley and Michael Dwyer, ed. *Great Houses of the Hudson River*. New York: Bulfinch Press, 2001, p.12-19.

Howard, Hugh (Roger Straus, photographer). *Houses of the Founding Fathers*. New York: Workman Publishing, 2007, p.156–167.

Rath, Fred L., ed. *Schuyler Mansion: A Historic Structure Report*. Albany, NY: State Division for Historic Preservation Bureau of Historic Sites, 1977.

Reisem, Richard (Andy Oelnick, photographer). *Historic New York: Architectural Journeys in the Empire State*. Rochester, NY: Landmark Society, 2006, p.88–91.

Proprietary House:

Randall, Willard S. *"The Proprietary House in Amboy."* Perth Amboy, NJ: Proprietary House Association, 1975.

WALLPAPER HISTORY:

Dagnall, H. *The Tax on Wallpaper 1712–1836*. Edgware, England: self-published, 1990.

Dow, George Francis. "Wall Paper" in *The Arts & Crafts of New England, 1704–1775, Gleanings from Boston Newspapers*. Topsfield, MA: The Wayside Press, 1927.

Entwisle, Eric A. *The Book of Wallpaper*. London: Arthur Barker, 1954.

Fowler, John, and John Cornforth. *English Decoration in the 18th Century*. Princeton, NJ: Pyne Press, 1974.

Hamilton, Jean. *An Introduction to Wallpaper*. London: Victoria & Albert Museum, Her Majesty's Stationery Office, 1983.

Kainen, Jacob. *John Baptist Jackson: 18th c. Master of the Color Woodcut*. Smithsonian Institution, Washington, DC: Government Printing Office, 1962.

Lefko, Linda Carter. "The Art of Grisaille Painting." *Early American Life*, April 2011, p.10–21.

Nylander, Richard C. "An Ocean Apart: Imports and the Beginning of American Manufacture" in *The Papered Wall*, Lesley Hoskins, ed. London: Thames & Hudson Ltd., 1994, p.114–121.

Oman, Charles C. "Part 1" in Oman, C., and Jean Hamilton. *Wallpapers: An International History and Illustrated Survey from the Victoria & Albert Museum*. New York: Harry N. Abrams, 1982, p.9–61.

Rosoman, Treve. *London Wallpapers: Their Manufacture and Use 1690–1840*. London: English Heritage, 1992. Revised ed., 2010.

Saunders, Gill. "The China Trade" in *The Papered Wall*. Lesley Hoskins, ed., London: Thames & Hudson Ltd., 1994, p.42–55.

Saunders, Gill. *Wallpaper in Interior Decoration*. London: Victoria & Albert Museum, V&A Publications, 2002.

Sugden, Alan, and John Edmondson. *A History of English Wallpaper 1509–1914*. London: B.T. Batsford Ltd., 1915.

Teynac, Francoise, Pierre Nolot, and Jean-Denis Vivien. *Wallpaper: A History*. New York: Rizzoli, 1982.

Thornton, Peter. *Authentic Decor. The Domestic Interior: 1620–1920*. New York: Viking Penguin, 1982.

Watkins, Walter Kendall. "The Early Use and Manufacture of Paper-Hangings in Boston." *Old-Time New England*, vol.12, January 1922, p.109–19.

Wells-Cole, Anthony. "English Manufacture 1680-1830" in *The Papered Wall*, Lesley Hoskins, ed. London: Thames & Hudson Ltd., 1994, p.22–41.

Wells-Cole, Anthony. *Historic Paper Hangings*. Temple Newsam Country House Studies, number 1. Leeds: City Art Galleries, 1983.

www.wallpaperscholar.com

PAINT HISTORY:

Bristow, Ian. *Interior Housepainting Colours and Technology, 1615–1840*. New Haven: Yale University Press, 1996.

Moss, Roger W. (ed.) *Paint in America: The Color of Historic Buildings*. Washington, DC: National Trust for Historic Preservation, 1994.

STATISTICS – POPULATION & WEALTH

Anonymous. *List of Inhabitants of the Citty [sic] of Albany*. November 1756, for John Campbell, Fourth Earl of Loudon. (Original handwritten document in the Lord Loudon Papers, Huntington Library, San Marino, CA; copy in New York State Library, Albany, NY.)

Benton, Josiah Henry. *Early Census Making in Massachusetts, 1643–1765*. Boston: Charles E. Goodspeed, 1905.

Dow, George Francis. *Two Centuries of Travel in Essex County Massachusetts: 1605–1799*. Topsfield, MA: Perkins Press, 1921.

Pruitt, Bettye Hobbs, ed. *The Massachusetts Tax Valuation List of 1771*. Camden, ME: Picton Press, 1998, 2nd printing.

LEE PORTRAITS:

Barratt, Carrie Rebora, and Lori Zabar. *American Portrait Miniatures in the Metropolitan Museum of Art*. New Haven: Yale University Press, 2010.

Kornhauser, Elizabeth. *American Paintings Before 1945 in the Wadsworth Athenaeum*. New Haven: Yale University Press, 1996.

Rebora, Carrie et al. *John Singleton Copley in America*. New Haven: Yale University Press, 1995.

THROUGHOUT THE COLONIAL TOWN'S TWISTING, curving streets, "very craggy and crasey" as one visitor wrote in 1750,[115] Marblehead has one of the largest concentrations of pre-Revolutionary houses in America.[116] Some are very fine, with stylish architectural details, like the Glover house, pictured on page 50, and many others are much more vernacular, like the one pictured above, with the eighteenth-century "red ensign" flag of Great Britain and her colonies, including those in America until 1775.

A MANNERIST FACE peers out from among rococo flourishes in an original painted wallpaper panel over the doorway to the large best parlor on the first floor. *MMHS*

PHOTO CREDITS

Thanks to the Marblehead Museum & Historical Society, the Lee Mansion's owner since 1909, for permission to reproduce images of the mansion interiors, which also include some of the museum's outstanding collection of furnishings and paintings that have been donated since the historical society's founding in 1898.

All photographs of the Lee Mansion and its interiors and wallpapers are by the author, unless otherwise indicated.

The individuals below generously provided additional photographs:

Rick Ashley, Marblehead (3)   Lucinda Lambton, London (1) (and cover photo)
Geoffrey Gross, New York (3)   Alex McLean, New York (1)
D. Bruce Greenwald, Marblehead (2)   Robert J. Mussey Jr., Boston (1)
Marcia J. Hunkins, Marblehead (2)   T. K. McClintock, Somerville (12)

Dennis Curtin—aerial view of Marblehead from the tower of Abbot Hall, 1876 (Marblehead town offices)

See also a photographic book produced by the MMHS with large-format photographs by Rick Ashley.

The following museums, individuals, and other organizations provided images for this publication:

Marblehead Museum & Historical Society   Marblehead Historical Commission

Cape Ann Museum, Gloucester, MA   Wadsworth Athenaeum, Hartford, CT
Schuyler Mansion, Albany, NY   Metropolitan Museum of Art, New York, NY
Albany Public Library, Albany, NY   Cooper-Hewitt, National Design Museum, New York, NY
New Jersey State Archives, Trenton, NJ   Board of Proprietors, Proprietary House at Perth Amboy, NJ
Historic New England Archives, Boston   Historical Society of Old Newbury, Newburyport, MA
Massachusetts Historical Society, Boston Colonial Williamsburg Foundation, Williamsburg, VA
British Museum, London   Museum of London

Adelphi Paper Hangings, NY   John Buscemi, Belfry Historic Consultants LLC, Lynn, MA
Prudence Fish, Gloucester, MA   Danny Recoder, Christopher Norman Collection, New York, NY
Dr. Keith Taylor, Marblehead, MA   Vincent McGrath, Marblehead, MA

NOTES

Marblehead Museum & Historical Society
Owner of Jeremiah Lee Mansion since 1909
www.MarbleheadMuseum.org/LeeMansion

1. Heckscher, *American Rococo*, p.20.

2. The artist of these full-size copies is thought to be Spencer Harding of Boston, brother of the more famous Chester Harding (the latter by family tradition and published by a descendant in 1916, but reconsidered by Narcissa Chamberlain (MHS) based on research after discussions with the Lee family donors in the 1960s, accdg. to notes in MMHS files). The original portraits passed down through the oldest daughter of the Lees' eldest daughter, Mary Lee Tracy (presumably after the death of her eldest son, to whom they were bequeathed by Martha Lee in a codicil to her 1791 will). They were on loan to the Museum of Fine Arts in Boston for 50 years until purchased by the Wadsworth Athenaeum in 1945. For information about the originals, see Rebora, *Copley in America*, 1995 and Kornhauser, *American Portraits*, 1996.

3. Many frames for portraits by J.S. Copley were carved by John Welch of Boston (see Heckscher, *American Rococo*, p.137-142), including a full-length portrait of Thomas Hancock very similar to Lee's (see Kornhauser, p.263 and note below).

4. The two other full-length portraits by Copley are of Nathaniel Sparhawk, a timber merchant in Kittery, Maine (Museum of Fine Arts, Boston), inspired by fully standing portrait of his father-in-law Sir William (painted after the latter was knighted for service in Canada at the Siege of Louisburg in 1745) (see notes 16, 22, 76), and merchant Thomas Hancock, the wealthiest man in Boston (uncle of his more famous heir, John, who commissioned the portrait for Harvard College, its current owner, upon his uncle's death in 1764). The compositions of Hancock's and Lee's portraits were similar, and likely modeled after a mezzotint portrait of the English queen Caroline, wife of George II, by John Faber Jr., 1739, from a 1736 oil portrait by John Vanderbank, whose full-length image included the same table seen in both men's portraits. See Rebora or Kornhauser.

5. Frangiamore, *Antiques Magazine*, December 1977 and Anderson, *Antiques and Fine Art*, Summer/Autumn 2009.

6. Born in 1721, Jeremiah came to Marblehead at about age 21 with his father, Samuel, a retired justice of the peace, from Manchester, MA on Cape Ann, farther up the seacoast north of Salem, whose harbor lies along Marblehead's northwest shore. Four years later, in 1745, both Lee and his recently widowed father married into two of Marblehead's most esteemed families (Hooper and Swett), linking them with prominent merchants in the town's extensive fish trade. A biography about Jeremiah Lee is in preparation; a 1916 biographical article has flaws that continue to be reiterated.

7. In 1765, when a detailed census was taken for the entire Massachusetts province, Marblehead's population was 4,954 people, with 935 families in 519 houses. Benton, Early Census 1765, p.76. (Nearby Salem had 4,254 people and Boston 15,520 while Newburyport had 2,882 – all more than Concord with 1,564 people and Lexington at 912.)

8. Of the Lees' 9 children, 6 survived infancy: Joseph, Samuel, Mary, Martha, Abigail, Jeremiah. Three married and had children. The youngest daughter was apparently officially betrothed, but the young man was lost at sea before they married and she died shortly after their daughter was born. (The birth of children after betrothal but before marriage was not uncommon or egregious in that American generation.) Due to the post-Revolutionary economies of Marblehead and Newburyport, the families faced financial hardship, and only a few grandchildren married. Space precludes further information; publication in progress.

9. The term "mansion house" was common for fine houses like this one. It was specifically noted as such on its first resident's probate inventory (d.1742) and that of the Lees' eldest son, Joseph (d.1785),

who had grown up in this house with his siblings until he left home for Harvard c.1764, (class of 1767/8). After Joseph married in 1771, he again lived in his childhood home with his wife and four young children, until his own early death at age 37. Early in the Revolution, 1775-6, Joseph was a captain in the Marblehead militia, in which his late father had served as colonel for a quarter of a century before.

10. Over a 3-month period in spring 1767, Col. Lee purchased a total of 589 board feet of mahogany from Salem cabinet-maker Nathaniel Gould, noted in one of the latter's account books, recently discovered in the Mass. Hist. Soc. by researchers Joyce King and Kemble Widmer. Two other early colonial stair-halls with mahogany paneling are known: Hunter House in Newport, RI (Newport Preservation Society of Newport County, RI, added in the 1760s from an earlier house that had a fire) and Westover (private home, along James River in Virginia); a parlor survives in Quincy, south of Boston, in the home of U.S. president John Adams and family 1788 to 1927 (National Park Service) from a c1749-65 remodel of a house first built in 1731 by Leonard Vassall.

11. Comment to author by Dr. Bernard Herman, formerly professor of American Studies at the University of Delaware, now at UNC Chapel Hill; and by others. The chimney-breast ornament replicates plates 51 and 53 in an English pattern book first published in 1745 by Abraham Swan, *The British Architect*, or *The Builder's Treasury of Stair-Cases*. For illus. of plate 51 (LI), see Heckscher, *American Rococo*, p.6; for a photo of the chimney breast, see same, p.19 (b&w) or Howard, p.60 (color). The carving on pendant drops alongside the chimney-breast is virtually identical to applied carvings in King's Chapel in Boston from 1754, by William Burbeck (unpublished observation by the author).

12. The only furnishings in the house that were once owned by the Lee family are ten side chairs from an unusually large set of "24 leather bottom" dining chairs, probably from this room, donated by Lee descendants who still retain some of the other chairs, including the matching arm chairs.

13. The glass remained in a house in Newburyport that had been home to Nathaniel and Mary Lee Tracy, eldest of Lee's three daughters; it descended through the families of subsequent owners after the house was sold, until donated to the historical society.

14. The stair brackets replicate plates 33 & 39 in *The British Architect* pattern book by Abraham Swan. (see note 11)

15. Wallpaper panels to cover fire-boards and for the space above an interior door and below a ceiling cornice were a popular component of the wallpaper manufacturing business. See McClelland, p.220. Wallpaper was also used to line books and small boxes.

16. Architectural papers, most appropriate for stair-halls, but used in other rooms too, were also available in block-printed versions, with either small- or large-format scenes with very large image repeats; those were more expensive than popular so-called 'pillar-and-arch' patterns (see note 76) but were less costly than hand-painted papers. A printed architectural paper survived behind a large painting in the entryway of an elegant house in Kittery, Maine, built in 1760 for the widow of Sir William Pepperell (see note 4) until 1945, when the paper was destroyed by a fire. Photo in Nylander et al; see p.51-54. For panorama papers, see Teynac, p.27-34.

17. See Dow, *Arts & Crafts*, p.150. In the 1700s, printed papers could be referred to as stained, stamped, or painted (as in quote cited). Most landscape mural papers were printed later, after the Revolution, and principally though not exclusively in France. See Teynac, p.27-34, Kosuda-Warner, chapter 1, and Saunders, *Interior Dec.*, p.89-95. The estate of a "stainer," settled in Boston in 1734

also likely referred to a wallpaper printer. (Wallpapers were not generally made in America until after the Revolution, though another wallpaper printer worked in Philadelphia beginning in 1739.) For early wallpaper production, see Nylander "An Ocean Apart" p.114-121, Lynn, p.107-113, Oman, p.9-61, Teynac, p.121, Watkins, p.109-119, Cummings essay in Nylander et al, p.3-27, and Rosoman 2010.

18. *London Evening Post*, 1752 (April 30-May 2), cited by Jacob Kainen in Jackson, p.33. In 1737, Boston merchant Thomas Hancock ordered a "shaded hanging" to be created his new stone house (unique in colonial New England) on Beacon Hill (destroyed 1863), from a pattern he had sent to England, requesting it be "well done" but "as Cheap as Possible" then adding a request for landscape scenes, in a description now iconic for the study of early wallpaper in America: "If they can make it more beautiful by adding more Birds flying here and there, with Some Landskips at the Bottom, Should like it well." He further implied that he felt the wallpapers seen more and more often in the city's homes to be "handsomer and better than Painted hangings done in Oyle…" (quoted in Watkins, p.110, Lynn, p.104, and most fully in Sanborn, p.62).

19. A 1761 trades guide by John Collyer stated that young entrants to the paper-hanging business would be expected to know how to draw and paint and have an eye for perspective. (Wallpaper grants *Case Statement*, MMHS archives)

20. Distemper is a light wash comprised of water and lime or chalk (or sometimes white lead) combined with a gelatinous size or glue as a binder, sometimes with pigment materials such as minerals or other compounds ground into it by hand for color. See Bristow or Moss.

21. The ambiguous word "tripolys" (after "10 Paintings of ruins of Rome" and "9 Ornaments of Pannells") on a 1761 invoice for papers purchased by Philip Schuyler of Albany seems to have referred to the decorative still-life clusters seen in the Lee and Van Rensselaer mansions, generally called "trophies."

22. A wallpaper in early America that imitated a "print room" with small images in simulated frames with decorative connecting motifs was formerly in the hall (parlor) of the 1760 Lady Pepperell house in Kittery, Maine, printed in grey on a pink background; a surviving piece is in the Historic New England coll. See note 16 and Nylander et al, p.51-53. For discussions of "print rooms" see: Little, p.96-105; Saunders, "Print Rooms" in *Interior Dec.*, p.82-87; and Wells-Cole in *Papered Wall*, p.38-39. A variant was in the Moffatt-Ladd house, 1763, in Portsmouth, NH, where engravings of sport hunting scenes based on paintings by a popular English sporting artist, James Seymour (1702-52) and individually printed on wallpaper paper, "traditionally formed a frieze at the cornice level." See Nylander et al, p.46-47. Eleven surviving prints were incorporated into an installation with a reproduction of the original geometric wallpaper. See www.moffattladd.org/collections.

23. For a list of the scenes, painters and engravers of the source images, see appendix D.

24. Narcissa Chamberlain, notes in MMHS files.

25. Original in N.J. State Archives. See Randall, p.16, illus.p.31.

26. "It is the papers…that bring the Lee house well into the mainstream of contemporary taste in Europe, where the fascination for ruins was at its peak, encouraged by such publications as … Piranesi's *Della Magnificenza ed Architettura de Romani* of 1761." Hall, *Country Life*, p.148.

27. Donnell, p.92-93, 100-1. Attribution to de Machy was made in the 1980s by Helen Hall, formerly at the Museum of Fine Arts, Boston, who researched and advised the MHS prior to the Lee wallpaper conservation in the 1980s. For paintings by Pannini relating to these wallpapers, see Leandro Ozzola, Gian Paolo Pannini. Torino, Italy: Edizioni D'Arte e. Calanza, 1921.

28. See Donnell, p.86-90. In her conclusion on p.106, she declared that "although the two sets were made in the same shop, each is the work of a different paper stainer."

29. In the 1760s, when Marblehead's population was nearly 5,000 (second only to Boston for about a decade, until the Revolution – see note 7), the population of Albany was about 4000, up from 2000 in 1756 (*List of Inhabitants*). A traveler who visited both towns noted that Marblehead was ".... somewhat larger than Albany, but not so neatly or compactly built, the houses all of wood and the streets very uneven, narrow and irregular. It contains about 5,000 inhabitants and their commodity is fish...." Dow, *Travel*, p.64-65.

30. The Van Rensselaer mural papers were apparently featured just in the downstairs entry space, since the wallpaper from only one room was removed and donated to the Metropolitan Museum, and because the hand-drawn plan sent back with the papers includes only that one room (see Donnell, p.85), and the 1768 bill from Van Rensselaer's London trading firm Neate & Pigou noted "1 Case paper for his Entry." The possibility that the scenic murals in the Schuyler mansion also did not extend beyond the entry, into the upper stair-hall, is suggested by the nearly identical number of panels (ten) and ornaments (nine) for "1 Room" noted on his invoice for purchases (illus. *Rath*, p.15), compared to the number and size of available wall spaces. See also note 37.

31. Heckscher, *Preservation in the American Wing*, p.131 and Shelley, p.126. After being taken down in 1893, other parts of the house were incorporated into a fraternity house on the campus of Williams College in Williamstown, MA, supervised by the Van Rensselaer donor's cousin; that structure was completed in 1895 and demolished in 1973. See archives.williams.edu.

32. For more detail, see Peck, p.203 and Donnell 1931 & 1932.

33. For a photo, see back cover or title page (for Lee), and (for Van R.), p.26 or Donnell, p.82, fig.5.

34. The letter is quoted in Donnell p.77 and Peck p.202. The plan is illus. Donnell p.85 and Shelley p.128. Stephen Van Rensselaer II (1742-1769) died at age 27, just a year after his house was complete. The estate was inherited by his five-year-old son Stephen III, just as Stephen II had inherited the manor property at age five, when his own father, Stephen I, died in 1747.

35. Howard, p.156-167 and Reisem, p.88-91. The Schuyler Mansion Historic Site is administered by the NY State Office of Parks & Historic Preservation (http://nysparks.com/historic-sites). The Friends of Schuyler Mansion (www.schuylerfriends.org) is a not-for-profit educational corporation established by the NY State Education Dept. that supports the education programs and interpretive initiatives for the house, and helps to maintain it.

36. The handwritten "*Invoice of Sundries Sent to America*" noted "*bought [of -* meaning from] *William Squire.*" The 1760s, when all three sets of scenic papers were purchased, were also when houses with rusticated wooden exteriors were most in vogue.

37. The Schuyler invoice also lists prices paid for the papers and various decorative trim elements (illus. Rath, p.15; discussed Lynn, p.53-56). While possible that Schuyler's painted images were for just one room (most likely his entry, as in the Van R. manor), the spaciousness of the upper stair-hall (as in the Lee Mansion) does not rule that out as a potential location. The other wallpapers listed on that particular invoice would not have been as appropriate for an entry hall, and the many Schuyler papers include no other invoice for them. British historic interiors consultant Guy Evans posited that Schuyler's images were likely for just that lower room, and wrote that they might have been smaller than Van Rensselaer's, or perhaps even printed, creating more of a "print-room" effect (especially since "painted" could be used for printed papers). Evans, p.29 and verbally to the author. Intriguing to consider is the lower cost of 3 itemized components in Schuyler's purchase that seem to relate to the Lee and Van R. papers (Paintings, Ornaments & Tripolys) – which totaled £6.10.6 compared to Van Rensselaer's much higher £37.15.8½. Neither amounts included shipping or import tariff. However, Van R's purchase was 7 years later, in an economically volatile decade, and monetary values may have changed (warrants further investigation). For a discussion of "caffy" or "caffaw" papers see Lynn, p.53-54.

38. Rath, p.15 &18-25. Wallpapers discussed p.22-24.

39. Philip Schuyler (1733-1804) married Catherine Van Rensselaer, a "lady of great beauty, shape and gentility" while an officer in the French & Indian War. Their fifteen children were raised in their mansion in town and at a farm estate farther up the Hudson River. One of their daughters, Elizabeth, married Alexander Hamilton, the first Secretary of the U.S. Treasury; in 1804, after 24 years of marriage and eight children, he was killed in a duel by Aaron Burr, General Schuyler's successor in the New York State Senate, the same year the General, Elizabeth's father, died; Elizabeth lived another 50 years, dying in 1854 at age 97.

40. Randall, p.15-17. Franklin was the cherished illegitimate son of Benjamin Franklin, and often followed his father in professional positions, until their divided loyalties as the Revolution began caused the father to renounce his son, who favored solutions to the colonial problems through negotiation rather than war. Randall, p.14 & 19-20. Franklin's wife died while he was imprisoned; he left for England with other exiled Loyalists in 1782, and died there in 1813.

41. Lynn, p.56 and Donnell 1931, p.12.

42. "The scheme of framing wallpaper landscapes with wallpaper borders in imitation of stucco became an inexpensive 'substitute which in time became more fashionable than' the use of 'the original' material." Rath, p.22, citing Donnell 1931, p.16. Thomas Chippendale's *The Gentleman & Cabinet-Maker's Director* of 1762 illustrated designs for borders stamped (printed) to imitate stucco work that were smaller and less asymmetrical than, but similar in character to, the *trompe l'oeil* frames around the scenic panels in the Lee Mansion. See Saunders, *Interior Dec.*, p.38 & 84. Borders of actual *papier maché* still surround deep crimson wool flock wallpapers in a room that was the parlor of the home of the last royal governor of New Hampshire, John Wentworth, in Portsmouth, NH, now the office of the administrator of a nursing home. (For photos of reproduction gilt *papier maché* borders, see J. Thomas Savage. *The Charleston Interior*. Greensboro, NC: Legacy Publications, p.14 & 16-17.)

43. Some fine scenic mural papers from the later 1700s, after the Revolution, can be seen in historic houses in several eastern states, in a few museum collections, and in England, but they are generally French or Chinese papers (all colored). (see "Chinese Papers" in Lynn, p.99-106, and Saunders "China Trade") Impressive Chinese hand-painted wallpaper murals are in an 18th c. period room in Winterthur Museum in Delaware (see Lynn, p.62-63) and in Henry Sleeper's "Beauport" in Gloucester, MA (Historic New England). See Nylander et al, p.92. But other than in the Lee Mansion, no painted English mural papers from before American independence survive on their original walls, and no other large format painted mural papers appear to survive at all, besides in the American Wing of the Metropolitan Museum of Art in New York City.

44. In the 20th c., the Proprietary House suffered vandalism and vacancy until taken over by the State of New Jersey in 1967 and restored by the Proprietary House Association, a nonprofit support group. (www.proprietaryhouse.org)

45. See Randall, *Proprietary House*, p.18.

46. The Blackett family dollhouse is a miniature town house, made for a gentry family rather than aristocracy; true to that socio-cultural milieu, it "lacks the grandeur of the celebrated dolls' houses at Uppark or Nostell Priory." Evans, p.30.

47. Evans, *Cultured Elegance*, p.28.

48. Saunders, "Scenic Wallpapers" in *Interior Dec.*, p.89.

49. Photos of some of the Harrington House panels are shown in McClelland, p.146-7 and Donnell, p.88, 95, 97, 98 (when they were still *in situ*). They were described at length in Donnell 1932 and Evans, p.30. The sport hunting scene design sources for the Hickstead Place papers were likely based on engravings by James Seymour, as described in Little, p.102 (also when they were still *in situ*).

50. See note 51, below. For the attribution to William Squire, see Donnell 1932, entire article, and conclusion, p.106. The attribution to William Squire is based on a comparison of two different scenes that replicate the same source images in both the Van Rensselaer hall and the Lee Mansion. One is the south-west panel in the parlour chamber, after Vernet (the Lee panel is horizontal, but VanR. is vertical). See beginning of note 69, and Donnell 1931 & 1932 for designer information with images of the engraving (1932, fig.26) and the panels ('32: VanR. fig.25, Lee fig.27; '31: VanR. fig.5, Lee fig.6). The other is a large panel on the Lee stair landing, west, after Pannini (covered by the portrait of Martha Lee, both originally and now; see this book, p.40 and Donnell '32, p.86 for discussion (panel illus. fig.8, engraving fig.9). The panel only is shown more clearly in a vertical photograph by Frank Cousins, in the MMHS archives; also published as plate XLIII (incorrectly in reverse) in an early 20th c. book (photocopy of image only in MMHS files). Philip Schuyler's invoice notes ten "Paintings of ruins of Rome" and "6 Tripoly's" among the other wallpapers *Bought [of] William Squire.*" These two principal and related merchants from the same town might likely have obtained some of their goods from the same sources, and the matching Lee and Van Rensselaer scenes suggest that all three sets almost certainly came from the same manufacturer. See also note 70.

51. Lynn, p.55 & note 7 (re: trade card of paper stainer William Masefield in the British Museum, who advertised "Paintings of Landscapes, Festoons and Trophies"; illus. Sugden, fig.43). For a thorough assessment of wallpaper manufacturers in London, see Rosoman 2010.

52. See Donnell, p.77, illus.p.85 and Shelley, p.126-128, illus.p.128. A newly married young husband, Stephen Van Rensselaer received a letter from his powerful father-in-law, Philip Livingston, who advised concerning the scenic wallpaper order: "*the directions how*

to place the paper is in the Box & You must take special Care if You Open it to look at that it be putt up as You found it, with the Letter on the outside I opened it and think it very Handsome indeed . . . ." (in Met. Mus. of Art archives). No plan survives for the Lee Mansion. In fact, few records at all are known for the Lee house construction, furnishing, Lee's business or any aspect of the Lees' lives. Lee's papers and accounts were likely in the possession of his eldest daughter's husband, Nathaniel Tracy, executor of Lee's estate, rather than his eldest son, in service in the Revolution when his father died. (Few Tracy papers survive either, and none for the Lees' son; there is evidence of a fire at the Tracys' Newburyport house in 1782, but many times old documents simply don't survive.)

53. See Rosoman 2010, p.3-5. For a simple but thorough discussion of paper-making, see Brown, Rick, ed. *Paper Making in America 1690–1820s*, at www.historybuff.com. For information about early wallpaper paper, see Sanborn, p.2-34 and any of the wallpaper history references.

54. Lynn, p.32 and others. The sheets of paper used for wallpapers were usually about 28" long by about 19" or 20" wide, though they varied, and some were 23" wide 'elephant' sheets, as the Lee papers are. (The Van Rensselaer papers vary in size, averaging 17" x 21" with the largest about 21" x 27" Shelley, p.129) Borders ranged between 1 and 2 inches, and were seldom the very wide borders that came into fashion after the Revolution. All four border patterns from the Lee Mansion measure $1\frac{5}{8}$" wide.

55. An early assumption that London wallpaper printer John Baptist Jackson (c.1700–77) made the Lee and Van Rensselaer papers, published in 1924 by respected wallpaper historian Nancy McClelland, was refuted by Metropolitan Museum curator of prints, Edna Donnell, in 1932 (in *Met Studies*). She explained that Jackson manufactured papers that simulated engravings, printed by a roller press, and colored with inks based in "oyl," while the Lee and Van Rensselaer papers were hand-painted in tempera, a form of watercolor. (She also corrected a misunderstanding that the Lee papers were purchased at 11 Regent St., London, "which was not laid out until 35 years after..." see p.84.) In 1962, Smithsonian Institution curator Jacob Kainen indicated that Jackson's business venture foundered in 1756 (a decade before the Lee Mansion was built). While Donnell could demonstrate that the Lee and Van Rensselaer wallpapers were not by Jackson, she stated that "at the present time no clue as to their maker exists." The likely attribution to William Squire was published in 1980 by Catherine Lynn, p.54-55.

56. Paper hangers were part of the upholsterers' trade. For an excellent discussion, see Saunders, "Paperhanging" in *Interior Dec.*, p.38-39, Teynac, p.27-34, Sugden, p. 80-83, and Robert M. Kelly, *Historic Paperhanging Techniques: A Bibliographic Essay*, presented at 2011 International Preservation Trades Workshop, Lancaster, PA (p.1-3); posted at www.wallpaperscholar.com.

57. Those tax stamps correlated to the fees colonists were compelled to pay for legal or other printed documents—permits, commercial contracts, newspapers, wills, pamphlets, and even playing cards. The wallpaper tax began in 1712. See Dagnall 1990, *Wallpaper Tax* and Rosoman 2010, p.7-9.

58. *Marblehead Messenger* newspaper, 1895 (my thanks to Robert Booth, Jr., for this reference).

59. According to imprecise indications in early MHS records, scrollwork designs that suggested the former wallpapers were apparently painted directly on the walls of the lower stair-hall by Marblehead artisan Thomas Pitman, who had also made some repairs to the existing wallpapers on the upper level of the house in 1909.

60. The special order French wallpapers were designed and installed by the W. Perry Company of Boston in 1966.

61. The arched window is nearly 11 feet tall and more than 5 feet across, with 35 panes of English glass, mostly original, and all unusually large for that time (11"x18").

62. For example, wallpaper printer J.B. Jackson described appropriate papers for "saloons" (quoted in Oman, p.24). See also Mark Girouard, *Life in the English Country House: A Social and Architectural History*, New Haven and London: Yale University Press, 1978.

63. On Mrs. Lee's 1791 inventory, one of the rooms was identified as the "Hall Chamber," meaning the bedroom above the best parlor or "hall." (New England's Josiah Quincy, admiring the upstairs parlor in the grand residence of Miles Brewton in Charleston, SC in 1773, asserted that it was "*the grandest hall I ever beheld, azure blue satin window curtains, rich blue paper with gilt, machee borders, most elegant pictures, excessive grand and costly looking*

glasses etc." (quoted in J. Thomas Savage, *The Charleston Interior*, p.15. op. cit. note 42; see p.14 & 16-17 for photos of reproductions of the blue paper and gilt papier maché borders.)

64. In the photo, the swelled, or "kettle base" chest of drawers, as often worded at that time, was one of many gifts to the Lee Mansion from Louise DuPont Crowninshield in the 1930s-50s. Like most of the other furnishings now in the house, it was not owned by the Lees. It has recently been attributed to the Salem furniture shop of Nathaniel Gould by researchers Joyce King and Kemble Widmer.

65. Jeremiah Lee's probate inventory (in Massachusetts State Archives) lists "a full suit of yellow silk damask / curtains with bedstead & easy chair / 7 squabs window curtains expence &c" valued at more than £79, in addition to 5 carpets at nearly £22 together and one large one valued at £20,7, and even rarer for that date, carpeting, at £54 – most likely in this room. See note 66. The reproduction bed hangings and other yellow silk damask textiles in that room were handcrafted in 1996 by Nancy Barnard of Lincoln, MA.

66. The 91 yards of "carpet*ing*" listed on Col. Lee's inventory was unusual for its yardage amount and description as opposed to "carpets," since few homes even had carpets at that time, and virtually none are known to have had fitted carpeting before the 1780s/90s. (See Sherrill, Sarah B. *Carpets and Rugs of Europe and America*. New York: Abbeville Press, 1996.) A fitted carpet documented to before 1775 was in the "Palace" of the royal governor in Williamsburg, VA, indicating the social standing and level of wealth required to own one. However, if assumed to be a fairly conventional 27" wide, the carpeting would have fit the dimensions of the Lees' room (26 x 20½ ft.), and tack holes at the room's perimeter may be from the 18th c. rather than later (warrants further study; in the 1800s, the room served as a board room for the Marblehead Marine Insurance Company). Yard-for-yard, at 12 shillings per yard, the carpet*ing* was twice the value of one large carpet (69½ yds.) and his 5 carpets (totaling 72 yds.), all noted at 6 sh. per yard. At £54, the 8-year-old carpeting was considered nearly as valuable as a mahogany desk-and-bookcase with glass doors (£64); the largest carpet (probably Wilton, based on Mrs. Lee's inventory 16 years later) was one-third the value. The carpet sample is from a 1758 design by Anna Goldthwaite of England "for the weaver Mr. Parks." Remarkable in that the design was created by a woman, it is also the earliest known pattern for which the point papers actually exist. The sample is on loan from John Buscemi, proprietor of Belfry Historic Consultants, who supplies historically accurate reproduction fabrics for home and museum installations, and provided the design information.

67. Documentary evidence from the period indicates that some owners of great houses occupied a bedchamber that was not necessarily the very best one.

68. The other two were in stately houses in Cambridge from that time. One was originally the home of the Massachusetts colony's lieutenant governor before the Revolution; later it was the residence of Marblehead merchant Elbridge Gerry, later a signer of the Declaration of Independence, a Mass. state governor after the Revolution, and the nation's sixth vice president under James Madison, from 1812 until his death in 1814. It is now the residence provided for the president of Harvard University.

69. The green color is based on paint analysis in 1990 by the Society for the Preservation of New England Antiquities, now Historic New England.

70. Donnell attributed the image sources for the scenes in this room (all horizontal) to painter Joseph Vernet, engraved by Jean Jacques LeVeau (Donnell 1931 & 1932, p.92). In both articles, she compares the horizontal southeast Lee panel (illus.'31 fig.6 & '32 fig.27) and a vertical scene in the Van R. hall ('31 fig.6 & '32 fig.25) as both based on an engraving by LeVeau titled "Mont Ferrat" of fishermen below an aqueduct and waterfall in Sardinia ('32 fig.26). A scene in the Van Rensselaer mural papers (vert., illus.'32 fig.16) after an engraving by LeVeau (horiz., a view of the Gulf of Naples, '32 fig.15) after a painter Donnell calls La Croix, is also similar to the northeast Lee panel (horiz., this book, p.45). A third engraver named "Coulet" was also identified by Donnell, on a chart in the appendix of her 1932 article (p.107). The only engraver with that surname, to date, is identified in two sources as Anne-Philibert Coulet. (*A Dictionary of Universal Biography: of All Ages and of All Peoples* by Albert M. Hyamson, 1916 and *Dictionary of Painters and Engravers, Biographical and Critical* by Michael Bryan, 1816; author reference) In the 1816 source, a list of engravings by Coulet after European paintings included a suite of five paintings by Joseph Vernet, to whom Donnell attributed the painted originals; three of the four scenes in this Lee Mansion room could correspond to at least two of those titles: *Fishermen Throwing their Nets and Neapolitan Fishermen*. See also note 50.

A biographical entry in the same ref. states: "This ingenious French lady has engraved several plates of very pleasing landscapes and marines which are charmingly etched and finished . . . in a delicate and agreeable style..."

71. The pattern repeats were very large; some were actually larger than the three vertical feet that were saved and framed.

72. The six panels and additional smaller wallpaper pieces were catalogued in 1994-5 by Michelle Cutting, while still on staff at the MHS. The six panels, all in frames, had been discovered in 1982 in a storage location by the Society executive secretary, Bette Hunt, who had them unframed and archived; no notations as to their original locations were found, nor where the frames had hung. The circumstances of their removal are unknown, but the author, when Lee Mansion curator, formulated a possible hypothesis; contact her for further details.

73. In 1938, six fragments of a seventh pattern (illus.p.53, top) were donated to the Cooper Union Museum in New York City by Miss Grace Lincoln Temple, along with pieces of four other patterns from the Lee mansion that had been given to her by the president of the Marblehead Historical Society, Richard Tutt (according to Cooper-Union records), sometime after he assumed that position in 1921. The notes also stated that the pink floral wallpaper pattern was thought to have been in at least one of the three rooms of the Lee mansion's first-floor back parlor suite, whose largest room was long referred to as the "counting room." A small photo in the MMHS archives vaguely shows an unidentified wallpaper in part of that suite of rooms, which could be that paper (though it appears to be more striped), or perhaps a later wallpaper from the 1800s, or even, though less likely, an eighth original printed pattern that no longer survives. My thanks to Joanna Warner, former curator of wallpapers at the Cooper-Hewitt Mus., for details of the 1938 donation, and Gregory Herringshaw, current curator of wallpapers, for information and the photo.

74. Temple Newsam house in England is one in which many did (see Wells-Cole, Paper Hangings). The foremost collections of 18th c. English wallpapers are in The Victoria & Albert Museum in London, Temple Newsam in Leeds, The Whitworth Art Gallery in Manchester, and English Heritage. The principal collections of early wallpapers are at Historic New England, the Cooper-Hewitt National Design Museum in New York City, the Colonial Williamsburg Foundation in VA, and the Rhode Island School of Design in Providence, RI. In American homes, at least four entire rooms retain c.1760s-70s English wallpaper – all richly flocked floral papers in 2½-story houses: 1) a parlor with crimson floral paper, complete with its three-dimensional *papier maché* borders, in the Gov. Mark Wentworth house in Portsmouth, NH (now the office of a nursing home, not open to the public); 2) two rooms in the Wentworth-Coolidge mansion outside Portsmouth (state of NH); 3) a second-floor chamber with sparkling crimson rococo paper in the Sarah Orne Jewett House in S. Berwick, Maine (Historic New England) 4): a bedchamber in the Joseph Webb House in Wethersfield, CT, with crimson red wool flocked paper left in place because George Washington used the house as his headquarters for several weeks during the Revolution, and lodged in that room (Webb-Deane-Stevens Museum).

75. Conversation with John Buscemi, Belfry Historic Consultants, and a letter from a merchant establishment in Rhode Island complaining to their English supplier: "The paper hangings came without border, and are now laying useless." (Casey Papers, 22.317, Historic New England, in Nylander "An Ocean Apart" p.120) The Schuyler invoice included 80 dozen lengths of printed borders in addition to the 26 dozen "Stoco" borders. (See Saunders *Interior Decoration*, p.38 for image of a printed faux stucco border and Savage, op.cit. note 42, p.14, 16-17 for an image of reproduction gilt *papier maché* borders.)

76. An elaborate printed architectural pattern from a house in Chelsea, MA was reproduced by the Thomas Strahan Company, of Boston and Chelsea (no longer in business; the company's cylinder blocks were purchased by another firm) as a pattern called "The Cordova." (For an image, see http://thomasstrahan.com/products. html.) For a discussion of the simpler and more popular "pillar and arch" patterns, see Nylander et al, p.48-51, including photos of two examples no longer extant: in the stair-hall of the gambrel-roofed Nathaniel Sparhawk house in Kittery, Maine (demolished 1967; interior photo from the archives of Strawbery Banke Museum, Portsmouth, NH) and formerly in the Timothy Johnson house, N. Andover, MA (photo from Phillips Library, Peabody Essex Museum, Salem, MA, then Essex Institute; a long fragment is in the Historic New England coll.).

77. Major John Glover was promoted to Colonel of the Marblehead militia in May 1775, upon Col. Jeremiah Lee's unexpected death. After becoming a full regiment, it gained fame for its heroic

service under Glover's command (particularly for rowing Gen. Washington's Continental Army of 9,000 men plus oxen and equipment across the Long Island Sound for a retreat in August 1776 that saved the army, then in December across the ice-choked Delaware River on Christmas Night for the pivotal battle in Trenton, NJ), after which Glover was promoted to General. Glover's house, with its handsome front doorway portico and graceful central staircase, was built in 1761-2, soon after Glover—a smaller scale merchant and inn-keeper whose fortunes had risen along with Marblehead's, up from his earlier trade as a cordwainer making shoes—enlisted in the militia and joined the local Mason's lodge. The fragments from the General Glover house (HNE, 1967.28) can be seen in Historic New England's online wallpaper database (www. historicnewengland.org / collections /wallpaper/1700-79) along with a piece from the Timothy Johnson house (1926.960.1; see note 76).

78. Philip Schuyler ordered seven different colors of English flocked wallpapers for his Albany mansion (see Rath, p.15 & 22). Wallpaper was flocked with powdered textile shavings, often wool, blown from a bellows onto adhesive applied onto a pre-painted pattern. It is thought to have first been produced by about 1600 in France. See Saunders, *Interior Decoration*, p.55-62, McClelland p.52-52 & 56, Teynac, p.66-75, Wells-Cole "English Manufacture" and Nylander, both refs. Many flocked papers imitated cut velvets, and were very expensive; the reproductions installed in several rooms of the Schuyler mansion are that type. Other flock patterns, like the Lees', lacked the brushed texture, and simply looked like flock papers; those are, and apparently sometimes were, called "mock-flock."

79. Historic New England wallpaper collection online database (1934.407a,b, see note 77).

80. A crimson red flock with white highlights and mica flecks to make it sparkle is "one of the most elaborate" English flocked papers surviving in America (Nylander et al, p.42-43). It can be seen in a chamber of the 1774 Sarah Orne Jewett house in S. Berwick, ME (Historic New England).

81. The blue floral border that matches this paper is available in a reproduction through Adelphi Paper Hangings. (info note 89)

82. Note the border with the paper, which did not match it, nor was it even the same colors. Though customers desired borders, and preferred them to match, that was not always possible. See Lynn, p.137 and Saunders, *Interior Decoration*, p.37.

83. Observation related to the author in 1999 by Margaret Pritchard, curator of wallpapers at the Colonial Williamsburg Foundation (CWF), recorded in curatorial summary at MMHS.

84. This pattern is not represented in the MMHS collection. It was one of four patterns from the Lee Mansion donated to the Cooper Union Museum in 1938 (see note 73 for details). My thanks to Gregory Herringshaw, wallpaper curator at the Cooper-Hewitt, National Design Museum, for taking and providing this photo several years ago.

85. Technical pigment analysis at the CWF in 1999 revealed that this paper's original accent color was pink, rather than crimson or red that had faded over time. Pink was a popular color in the last half of the 1700s in Europe and England, and therefore in their colonies.

86. Information about the early 20th c. reproductions is from Lee Mansion House Committee annual and monthly board reports (brief and imprecise, as often happens in that context) in MMHS archives. For the Thomas Strahan Company pattern archive, see www.ChristopherNormanCollection.com.

87. For thorough discussions of *Chinoiserie* wallpaper, see all principal wallpaper history references.

88. That reproduction was first printed in 1999 at the Farmers' Museum in Cooperstown, NY, part of the New York State Historical Association, under the direction of Wendy Weeks, for installation in the Peyton Randolph house in Williamsburg, VA, commissioned by CWF. Wallpaper curator Margaret Pritchard consulted on the entire project: hand-drawing of the original patterns for the various wood blocks, carving of the blocks, analysis of original paint colors and composition, application of the pigments, and period-appropriate installation procedures. (see notes 83, 85)

89. The reproduction is currently available in several color-ways through Adelphi Paper Hangings (www.adelphipaperhangings. com), a company established in 1999 by Christopher Ohrstrom and Steve Larson, who had previously worked in a wallpaper printing workshop at the Farmers' Museum in nearby Cooperstown, NY. All their wallpapers are based on historically documented patterns,

paint colors are specially mixed, and printing is done by hand on a wooden press.

90. Conversations with wallpaper curators in America and England. Very small fragments with blue-green color that appears similar to this paper were recently found in the parlor of the home of Colonel James Barrett, outside Concord, MA, the leader of those to whom Jeremiah Lee was secretly shipping gunpowder and other supplies as the American rebellion mounted. Barrett's farm was also the destination of the British army in April 1775 when the battles of Lexington and Concord occurred, and was raided but not destroyed. Fragments found by Rick Detwiller of New England Landmarks, preservation consultant for Save Our Heritage, the non-profit organization restoring the house, now within the boundaries of Minuteman National Historical Park.

91. Why such a high-style pattern was installed in a third-floor hallway is perplexing. However, conservators determined that it did not appear to have been relocated to that area from a different room. It may remain *in situ* because in the mid-1800s, the eastern rooms of the house were inhabited by a large family (that of the Marblehead Bank's 'cashier,' who was responsible for the security of the cash deposits), so the third-floor green *Chinoiserie* papers on the western side may not have been impacted as negatively as the grey and pink pattern that had once been in the family's living spaces.

92. Analysis in 2005 by Susan L. Buck, PhD, nationally respected paint analyst and conservator of historic finishes in Williamsburg, VA, determined that the principal colors of this paper included "blue verditer" on the leaves, which would have created a blue-green tone, and "madder lake" with small amounts of lampblack and calcium carbonate, to create a red color on the lower garments and a rose red on the flowers. The principal border colors were madder lake and green verditer. (Recorded in wallpaper conservation treatment report of Studio TKM. A summary by the Lee Mansion curator lists the six patterns and their colors in a simplified manner. Both in MMHS files.) In simple terms, "verditer" was a carbonate derived from copper into which the mineral malachite was ground to create green verditer; azurite was added for blue. See Bristow or Moss.

93. The mid-1700s wallpaper found in 1915 was under a later lath-and-plaster wall; the paper had been applied directly onto wooden boards that formed the original interior wall. It was reproduced by the Thomas Strahan Company of Chelsea and Boston as "The Stanwood-Mansfield," as the house itself later became known, after its subsequent owners. See Prudence Fish, *Antique Houses of Gloucester*, The History Press, 2007, p.93. My thanks to Daniel Recoder, Vice President of Product Development, Christopher Norman Collection, 979 Third Avenue, Concourse Level, New York, NY 10022. (212) 644-5301. www. waterhousewallhangings.com

94. See drawing, page 31 in this book, top left room, "*Governor's Study or Office.*"

95. The 18th c. Chinese floral wallpaper was donated by Mrs. Louise DuPont Crowninshield specifically for that space. For a photo and description of an 18th c. 'closet' or small room for dressing or bathing in an aristocratic English house ("The Chinese Dressing Room" in Saltram house near Plymouth in Devon, England), see Lucinda Lambton, *Temples of Convenience*, New York: St. Martin's Press, 1995, p.40-41 (and many other varieties of privy rooms) or Saunders, "The China Trade" p.47.

96. The woodwork color was determined through analysis in 1984 by Morgan Phillips of the Society for the Preservation of New England Antiquities. Some paint specialists believe that the current color may appear more green than the original would have been. The tiles were from a manufactory begun by John Sadler in Liverpool, England, before his partnership with Guy Green, formed in the later 1760s, which created the more familiar company name "Sadler & Green"; one of the tiles, not illus., shows just the name "Sadler" in a corner.

97. "The Marblehead" was retailed locally by the Bixby Company in Salem, along with "The Canton."

98. "The Canton" was offered periodically in various Strahan Collections through the 1900s. It is available again through Adelphi Paperhangings (hand-block printed) and Waterhouse Wallhangings (digitally printed based on 20th c. surface printing techniques). A new reproduction will likely be installed in that area at some point, thanks to grants from the Society of Colonial Wars in the Commonwealth of Mass. matched by the General Society.

99. Viewed through magnifying scope, a tiny fragment of printed wallpaper still attached to a base-board at the top of the cupola stairs appears to be 18th c. paper, perhaps with a small bit of black vine like the pink and grey *Chinoiserie* pattern.

100. Known as the French & Indian War in America, it involved much of European-held America, Native American allies of England and France, and much of Europe, including Massachusetts' trading partners on the Iberian Peninsula (Portugal and Spain, see Appendix C), though to a lesser extent. Colonial taxes enacted in the 1760s to replenish of British financial losses from that war and to better control the Colonies economically were not the only reason for the rebellion that became a revolution for independence, but they certainly were sparks that ignited it.

101. Not long after his mansion was complete, Lee traveled to other colonies to advocate for revolution, moderated and codified Marblehead's official objections to British policy, was elected to the Provincial Congress (the Massachusetts colony's rebel legislative body), was selected by that group to present the colony's grievances to the king's military governor in Boston, trained for active duty with the militia he had led as Colonel for 25 years, and pursued a perilous secret effort to secure weapons for the impending rebellion on behalf of the Patriot cause.

102. There were, of course, other earlier acts of armed responses to what many perceived as tyranny by the mother country, England.

103. In his actions, Lee was committing treason against the Crown in three ways: trading in an illegal commodity (weapons), with one of England's traditional enemies (Spain), and challenging British government. Lee's trading agent in the port of Bilbao in northern Spain, near the Pyrenees mountains, was Guardoqui et Fils [and Sons], a prominent Basque family. A revealing letter written by Joseph Guardoqui on 15th Feb.1775 in response to Lee's queries about purchasing weapons from Europe survives in the Mass. State Archives (vol.193). It perhaps fortuitously arrived in after Lee left Marblehead on April 18th, for what proved to be forever, and was therefore not among Lee's other papers, which appear to be lost.

104. The war had nearly begun in Salem in February that year, just days after Lee's eldest daughter married one of the wealthiest young businessmen in Newburyport, but hostilities were avoided as the Salem and Marblehead militias confronted the British regular army troops, sent to confiscate weapons stored beyond Salem's North Bridge, as happened in Concord just two months later with a very different outcome. (It began in Lexington & Concord in April 1775.)

105. Author's curatorial hypothesis based on social and economic conditions in Marblehead, and primary source evidence related to that. After the first battles in April 1775, many coastal residents fled inland "to take shelter with any who would take them in," a Salem woman wrote in a letter, due to concerns about British reprisals. Later in April, a Marblehead diarist, Ashley Bowen, noted, "Most of our people moving." Limited space precludes further discussion; a biography of the Lee family is in preparation.

106. At some point, the women and youngest son in Lee's remaining family lived away from Marblehead, in Newbury and Newbury Port, where the three girls were married and betrothed. Most ended their lives in obscurity and near-poverty. For 20 years after the death of the colonel's only viable heir—his eldest son Joseph, in 1785 (see note 9)—title to the Lee mansion was held by three different men who never resided in it, or even in Marblehead: after Joseph's death, the mansion was transferred by indenture to the Lees' son-in-law Nathaniel Tracy (who had lost a significantly through providing and supplying privateer vessels to support the Revolution), then immediately to Tracy's creditor, John Cabot of Beverly; a year later, title was conveyed to Joseph Sheafe, a merchant in Portsmouth, NH, from whose heirs in London the house was purchased in 1804 by Mass. Samuel Sewall, Mrs. Lee's former attorney and a trustee of the newly formed Marblehead Bank. The trustees purchased the mansion a few months later for their new banking operations.

107. The satellite bank was established as the Marblehead Savings Bank, when the original bank became the Marblehead National Bank in both name and operation after U.S. lending laws changed in the 1860s. The newer bank is still in business, now as Marblehead Bank, recalling its parent that had started more than two centuries ago. (In 1831, a rival bank in Marblehead was established as the Grand Bank, named after the North Atlantic fishing banks that still supplied the town's principal livelihood at that time, that changed dramatically after 1846, when a devastating gale decimated the fishing fleet; that bank also became a national bank in the 1860s, and still operates independently as the National Grand Bank.)

108. The *Marblehead Messenger* newspaper noted that a low barrier was added to prevent ready access to the stairs and upper stair-hall. Evidence can still be seen in the mahogany wainscot rail.

109. Some damage was apparently also suffered by the 18th c. *Chinoiserie* papers in the north-south third-floor hallway outside the rooms where 19th c. political organizations met, since only the upper sections remain, in somewhat patched condition. (see pencil inscription in photo p.73).

110. Elsewhere on the plaster wall, small pencil sketches appear to be part of an 1830s chair and a carriage seat.

111. The glass panels were installed over all the remaining painted papers by Irving & Casson of Boston and NY City, funded by Louise DuPont Crowninshield.

112. See also Anderson, MMHS *Newsletter*, Summer 2006.

113. For a definition of stone colors see Ian Bristow, p.173.

114. Shoremen oversaw the curing of the salted fish as it was dried on the rocky headlands, on acres of wooden racks called "fences" or "flakes." They also outfitted the ship-owner's schooners with supplies and men, and served as a middleman between the owner or owners of a fishing schooner and the vessel master, who usually hired the crew. Shoremen made a comfortable living, owned fine houses, and often became owners or part-owners of vessels themselves. See Samuel Roads, *History and Traditions of Marblehead*. New York: Houghton Mifflin Co., 1881. My thanks also to Robert Booth, Jr. for his in-depth information about Marblehead records and history.

115. Ship captain Francis Goelet of New York City in 1750, cited in Dow, Travel, p.76. His journal is in the New-York Historical Society.

116. Other towns with a notable legacy of homes pre-dating 1775 are Annapolis, MD; Charleston, SC; and Newport, RI. In three towns north of Marblehead—Salem & Newburyport, MA and Portsmouth, NH—many colonial homes stand side-by-side with those towns' more famous Federal-period architecture, while Ipswich, above Cape Ann, is noted for the most houses built before 1725. In addition to countless individual colonial-period houses throughout the eastern U.S., concentrations remain in Glastonbury, CT, coastal RI towns, and others, but not in the numbers still seen in Marblehead.

Referring to the artisans who painted the scenic papers:

"These journeymen, who wrote no books, and discovered no new technical processes, although they lost their identity in a factory routine, still made their individual contribution to eighteenth-century decorative arts."

Edna Donnell, 1932
Department of Prints
Metropolitan Museum of Art

MMHS, Photo by T.K. McClintock

It was a privilege to work with the Jeremiah Lee Mansion for sixteen years, the last eight as its curator, for as long as the position existed; and I am grateful to be able to present this material in this book.

Judy Anderson